LANDFALL 201

UNIVERSITY OF OTAGO PRESS DUNEDIN

LANDFALL 201

Issue 201 May 2001

Editor Justin Paton
Production Editor Simon Cauchi
Design Aaron Richardson and Bepen Bhana, *designworks*
Founding Editor Charles Brasch (1909–1973)

Landfall is published in May and November. The subscription rates for 2001 (two issues) are: New Zealand $39.95 (including GST); Australia $A30.00; rest of the world $US30.00. Sustaining subscriptions help to support New Zealand's longest-running journal of arts and letters, and the writers and artists it showcases. Sustaining subscriptions are available in two categories. Friend: between $NZ75 and $NZ125 per year. Patron: $NZ125 and above.

Landfall publishes poems, stories, excerpts from works of fiction and non-fiction in progress, reviews, literary, social and cultural commentaries, articles on related arts, and portfolios by artists. Written submissions must be typed, with an accurate word count recorded on the last page, and accompanied by a stamped, addressed envelope.

The winner of the next *Landfall* essay competition will be announced in *Landfall* 203, May 2002. Entries will be accepted until December 21, 2001.

Send subscriptions or submissions to the address below. For subscription or editorial inquiries, or entry forms for the *Landfall* essay competition, call 64 3 479 8807 or email <university.press@otago.ac.nz>.

ISBN 1-877-276-80-4   ISSN-00-23-7930

© University of Otago Press 2001

Cover by Saskia Leek, from the portfolio *Underwood*

Published by University of Otago Press, 56 Union St, PO Box 56, Dunedin, New Zealand.

Typeset by Egan-Reid Ltd. Printed in New Zealand by Printlink Ltd.
Landfall is published with the assistance of Creative New Zealand.

designworks™

Uninterrupted views

Anne Kennedy

House on hill

From the house I saw wind, and saw six figures in the sky. They were blinding but then there was the outlook for Saturday, which was for fine weather. I just hung on until Saturday came, and then—guess what?—it was clear. Some people have a tender, spongy kind of vision that you'd think you could squeeze, but in fact you can't. Then it all gets played or recited or written down or something (i.e. it's gone). And all the great plans become plans. Once I heard birdsong which had been recorded and played backwards. Now there is something concrete. Notice I say 'is'. It outlasted the bird.

Coming to the place formerly known as home

and knowing every inch of the play area intimately, and smelling again the scorched sand near the sea wall, which manages to smell just the same as it used to. You'd think it would have changed, but no. And there is no sand as definitive as that sand, and no play area so pure. Those irksome twenty years close over. Was it better when the wound was fresh?

Grace Removals
(for Sally and Alan)

An inventory of contents would defy the moving company let loose like gas in
the theatrical household. A dotted line for masks, puppets, a row of costumes
with their shoulders to the room like the spines of books. What's their value,
taking into account wear and tear and the loudness of the applause? A copy of
Paterson more than five years old. Would Grace buy you a new one, for instance, if it fell off the truck, or scour the second-hand booksellers for a
replacement? There's also the filing box of juvenilia, the number of times you
crossed the room, and that single moment of being speechless, perhaps. The
time the sun dropped suddenly behind the hills and the sitting room stepped
over into night. Help. Our things are bubble-wrapped. We have no shelter.
Thank you.

Change brings prosperity to the superior man

The first change was the purpling of nipples and feeling the wind cold on them, the second change was knowing what the first change was. The third change was feeling sick and the fourth growing bigger, the fifth moving in together, and then I lost count of changes, except to know that cells in their young bodies change at the rate of knots, and that we are withering slowly. They changed schools, they changed friends, teachers, neighbours, streets, cities. Aue! We cling to the changes we know, rather than those we don't.

A bodkin, perhaps?

My lover and I had an urge to throw everything away, be unencumbered, this after seeing the film *The Cup*, and going straight to Borders afterwards and buying the words of the Dalai Lama. Somehow the message of the camel, the rich man and the eye of the needle had never sunk in so well. Also we were moving and came to the enlightened conclusion that possessions are simply too much trouble to pack. In the same vein we took on a sponsored child, a miraculous conception that occurred late one night in front of a TV ad. This child was in addition to our own $1-a-day pair (only joking, the cost of a good scooter is steep). Our first weekend at the local park a balloonish castle was fed a steady diet of air. The sign said 'No shoes or food.' What to do? Do you ply the charity and prop up the regime, or change the world, become a terrorist? I don't know. But there were no shoes, and there was no food either. The stirrings of the dormant sponsored child growing enormous might tip the planet sideways. Seriously, it could grow up able to buy fossil fuels like us. Ah, but no chance on $1 a day. There were no shoes or food as the children boinged up and down.

Indices

A few years ago I saw a woman wheeling a baby in a white carriage cocooned in silver like a nursery spider's web. She wheeled this shimmering thing beside the roaring Great North Rd and under the railway bridge. For some reason the word 'indices' came to mind. I remembered I had heard it in maths at school and totally ignored its meaning because it was, well, maths, but thought it a nice word. But why did it come back then? Was it to attach something to the sight of the woman and her baby? They're indexed under innocence or spiders or traffic, not forgotten, but I guess that baby's almost grown up now.

First and last times

The last walk to the school is walked as the first walk was, noticing every leaf, every crack, and Geigering the level of noise from the motorway. The last night in the house is slept as the first was, everything foreign and undone. The last trip to the supermarket is a little death. What to do with all the times in-between, passed now, and not first or last?

What I thought

I thought it was an aria (*Remember me, remember me*) but it was the sound of the washing machine on spin. I thought it was a pipe band but it was the siren of the police car heading down the parade. I thought it was the surge of the sea but it was a wistful memory of the north-western motorway. I thought it was the bells ringing out from St Joseph's, the Mrkusich church. It was Robert knocking on the door to the internet. I thought it was a child's sleeping breath curving out into the hall, but it really was the growly bear. I thought it was a fine night, but our daughter worried this wind was bad weather for fairies to be out in. If you hear these things, please, tell them where we are. I didn't just think, I knew it was the wind in the trees, and it was and it was, day and night, the big noise of moving air encountering tree. At least this much is true, Robert.

Constructed Comfort:
Fort/House

Ellen Brooks

The act of fort-making is an initial assertion of spatial dominance and self-definition. The fort structure is a refuge charged with a psychological and visceral dimension, an environmental narrative describing a 'primary architecture'. Children make hideouts. They make small enclosures for themselves within the larger parameters of tamed environments, securing and refining private realms. Their houses are sites of autonomy and independent exploration enacted within a protective confinement. The fort surrounds the child, sustaining but self-made. This is a place of comfort and security, but also of concealment and separation. This is where private, secret and forbidden thoughts and acts can be dared.

—Ellen Brooks

JAMES NORCLIFFE

George's shirts

1

were of softest lawn
and always white

they billowed with
the gentleness of feathers

and when they were ironed
they steamed with the longing

of George's cologne

2

their double cuffs
were made to shoot

elegantly from the buttons
of his pinstriped jacket sleeves

the links of black onyx
shone like antelope eyes

like George's longing

3

George's shirts hung
in my closet like a benediction

their sleeves fell
in supplication

I reached into them
and entered them blindly

brushing aside George's fingers

planchette

at night the rats
are bigger than rats

they race back and forth
like typewriters
across the lath and plaster

like good little rats
they have taken their poison
and now they grow large with thirst

where are their pretty girlfriends
or love, the magician?

can not one of these
offer them solace or slake?

oh qwerty they clatter
oh qwerty qwerty

as the night grows hard around them
desperate in their scrabble

and the stars
set like teeth

In the Lock-Up

Damien Wilkins

BIOGRAPHY'S EYES are always bigger than its stomach. It has a voracious appetite but it swallows little of what it puts in its mouth. As readers of biography, feeding off its gains, we can feel simultaneously full and empty. *Wrestling with the Angel*** is an important book, instructive in many ways, sympathetic and careful—a required work in fact; it is also a bit unsatisfying and toneless. It lacks, finally, I think, an internal auditor for the often remarkable things it places before us, a discerning presence to guide us through the texts of a literary life—letters, novels, poems, reviews, interviews—someone who registers in these written and spoken things not simply an itinerary but an interior.

James Fenton has warned that all biography is in a way pretentious, since we can truly know so little of even the people to whom we are closest. Measured against this somewhat half-hearted injunction—Fenton was himself writing an introduction to a biographical work—Michael King is the least pretentious biographer around, for the simple fact that he does not attempt a personality. He hugs facts not feelings, he counts votes but does not cast one, he repeats stories but does not fully find his own.

Partly this is a problem of the biography of the living writer where current sensitivities obscure the view. Frame's relationship with Bill Brown and Paul Wonner, for instance, clearly awaits another venue for the full story to emerge. For now we have the teasing quotes from Frame's lovely letters with which to piece the action together:

I couldn't stay with you any longer because I was so lonely at night, not being able to snuggle up to you both occasionally. I've already trained for death in that direction. Anyway, I'm sorry that I embarrassed you by anything I said, say, did, do, imply or desire.

King's commentary via Wonner and Brown? The two men had decided 'they were unable to offer her the degree of intimacy for which she had hoped.'

Now for many readers, wary of more speculative biographies where intimacy is a form of presumption, the qualities here will come as a relief. The cleanness and clarity of King's book, its modest aims and excellent organisation, its judiciousness and its calm are not inconsiderable achievements. Its very presence—a serious scholarly life of a contemporary New Zealand writer, this writer especially—amounts to a force for good in our culture. Mark Williams has written that this book is 'unimpeachable'. I know what he means. But, then again, I don't. Once we've moved past our astonishment and gratitude at its existence, there are questions for us—questions about Frame and her achievement over which, despite the athletic title, the biography does not exercise itself. And questions about King, a historian, as our resident biographer of writers—his life of Frame follows on from his Sargeson.

Why have the novels of our greatest living writer been so divisive? Are her books uneven across that career or are they always uneven—uneven within themselves? Characteristically uneven, perhaps? (Patrick Evans, thirty years ago, wrote a monograph for students on Frame in which he roughed up the novels quite badly. Students looking for reassurance must have been bewildered. The strongest

---

* *Wrestling with the Angel: A Life of Janet Frame*, Michael King (Penguin, 2000) 583 pp., $49.95.

endorsement of Frame as a novelist 'in world class' comes in a two-page introduction from the publisher. Evans, of course, subsequently became interested in writing the biography—an interest which raises the same question King's book raises: if the books are such compromised creations, what are we all doing here?) Why, as a near-recluse, has Frame ended up publishing three books on the first half of her life, then sanctioned the film adaptation of those books? Is it the life, or the interpretation of that life, which is finally Frame's greatest achievement?

I don't intend to go very far into these questions here, but I do want to look at some of the ways King avoids his own entry into the life he now knows more about than anyone except the person living it.

A long time ago, Janet Frame ceased to be a writer and became a cultural 'effect'—a marker of something beyond herself. To be in the same auditorium as her was to look on an individual but also an emblem. The emblem had a lot to do with survival. You couldn't purchase immunity from this effect through any cool critical apparatus or even by being an outsider. The Canadian writer, Timothy Findley, wrote of Frame's reading at the 1986 Festival of the Arts: '[she] is a source of light and energy impossible to resist.'

In this elevation, naturally, we leave behind the actual—the person and her work. While King restores the everydayness of Frame—her problems with noisy neighbours, her colds and flus, her bank balance—my suspicion is that this biography is part of that cultural effect rather than its interrogation. Furthermore, I'd argue that at the core of King's

admired biographical ease lies his own diffidence to Frame's work. He moves with confidence through the life because the work is seen lightly. It is not hostility that is the problem but neutrality, and it's catching. The great piety of biography—that it serves the writer by sending the reader to her books—seems even more wishful than ever.

Around this point, however, there is a dispute.

In the Author's Note, King writes that Frame had a preference 'that it not be a critical biography (analysis of her writing)'. Frame has said in an interview following publication that this was not the case; there was no preference expressed. Whatever the truth, it's hard anyway to imagine King in the position of persuasively assessing the novels. And yet that is precisely what we need with Frame. The roll-call of reviews, whose meagre critical width is scissored even further into quotes, only serves to blur her status more completely.

King, in the interests of historical accuracy I suppose, samples a range of reviews, the mixed, the positive and the dismissive. The effect is to render each book, with the exception of the autobiographies and *Faces in the Water*, a sort of nil-all draw. (For me, these *are* Frame's great works, so maybe King is on to something after all.)

When King himself is drawn to make a comment, he endorses a review by Frame's friend Dennis McEldowney: 'It is almost impossible to judge a Janet Frame novel. Her books simply *are*, they arbitrarily exist (with whatever pains they are created) . . . *Intensive Care* is a characteristic Janet Frame experience.' This is a peculiar kind of non-criticism indeed but it suits the biographer's brief perfectly.

It is not a definitive judgement we require but a sense of the progression of the writer's work, a feel for the highs and lows of her art, a grid of strongly argued opinions against which we can test our own. Assembling newspaper reviews of the time gives the flavour of the times but not necessarily of the books. It shuts them off from our current gaze and makes them of a piece with their periods.

That its subject has written three extraordinary volumes of autobiography helps us see not only the obvious—that Frame's language is alive to a degree that King's is not—but also that biography can reduce the potency of a life. Often in the biography a flame of reasonableness is placed under incidents familiar to us from the autobiographies, until a vapour comes from the prose. This is the alcohol of confession being disappointingly boiled off.

In the first week of primary school, Frame steals money from her father's clothes. *To the Is-Land* devotes three pages to the event and its consequences. Here is King's paragraph:

> For Janet, though, the most unpleasant experience occurred in February 1930, a week after she had joined her older sister and brother in the primary department of Wyndham District High School. The infant teacher, Miss Ethel Botting, exposed 'Jean' Frame as a thief after she had taken money from her father's trouser pocket and bought chewing gum for members of her class. In an exercise of the kind of sadism not uncommon in schools at that time, Janet was made to stand in front of the desks for almost a whole day until she confessed. Miss Botting then 'gave the news to the class and it spread quickly around the school that I was a "thief" . . . [I was] appalled by my future prospects.'

Behind the bland concision ('unpleasant experience') one can readily intuit the pressure of the life—all those years, all those other events, in a holding pattern above the biographer's head. And yet there's something else to notice here—the emphasis King gives to the story. 'In an exercise of the kind of sadism not uncommon in schools at that time . . .' In any of the inflamed anecdotes Frame supplies, King is likely to put his fingers to the historian's itch and leave the more interesting and troubling spots alone.

The biographer is of course always mindful of a social context. We should grant him his patch. There are other things, however, we might find more representative in the tale as Frame tells it than to make Jean the victim of generalised forces. She has, of course, stolen the money. The appellation then is correct— she is a thief, and, in denying it and making up a story, she is also a liar. There is something commonplace about these offences in a young child, but to assign it, as King does, to the education system is to smother the nuances.

For King the story seems to place itself in a line of hurts, with Janet as the wronged party. While there is something stubborn and heroic in little Jean's refusal to confess—it's what makes us respond initially to the incident in the autobiography; that and our approval of her generosity in distributing the chewing gum among her classmates—our cheers also have another source. She is kept in front of the class through the whole day—which may well be sadistic—but she is, too, the agent of her own imprisonment. She can at any moment free herself with a word. This is also childhood's familiar bind, when, at the edge of our rages against adult conspiracies, we're given a useless glimpse of our own complicity. We feel our pain is searingly real but also that it is theatrical. Our recall of this rent in our consciousness adds another thickness to the telling. It's typical, we say, of childhood. More than this, we feel it's typical of Frame. The fix she's in, with its shadings of humiliation, defiance, creativity and shame, feels consistent. That is, like the best fiction, it suggests itself and also speaks to a future, reading backwards and forwards at the same time.

Wonderfully, Frame the adult writer, in that weird mix of childlike and mature diction which is her characteristic prose move, draws out the moment of capitulation, '. . . when the light was growing thin with masses of dark tiredness showing behind it, and the schoolroom was filled with a nowhere dust, and a small voice answered from a scared me . . .'

It is not injustice that haunts this anecdote but consequence. It's also consequence of a special kind—not that of immediate physical punishment, but of reputation. 'I'd been found out as a thief. I was so appalled by my future prospects that I don't remember whether Miss Botting strapped me.' She remembers the changing light and the nowhere dust but not whether she was strapped. There is a rightness to that. We feel the Frame memory, which is everywhere immense and fierce, completed somehow through its failures and gaps. What is not recalled, paradoxically, gives the life its life.

This lesson in lessness is not one that biography, with its hunger, its hoovering of every tidbit, can hear very well.

And there are still further notes to the story of Jean and the money that seem to offer ways into the life. She steals the coins 'brought back from the war', and tries to buy sweets with Egyptian currency. She must then lie to the shopkeeper when he points this out to her. ('"I know," I lied.') As we read on through the autobiography, we come to recognise such moments as 'vintage'—they denote *qualities* not simply happenings—and we understand that in these rich miniatures—presentiments—of her own later actions, Frame has found a way to suggest her essential self and its difficult relations with the world. There will always be a shopkeeper; she will always have Egyptian money.

King is certainly not lacking alertness when it comes to using Frame's own words to tell the story. He quotes often and well from her letters (now *that* would be some book). There are wonderful, assured letters about writing ('The last thing I ever want to be is literary') and brilliantly commanding character studies ('She was not an immediate person; there was a porch, an entrance hall where one waited to be received'). And there are terrifying, accusing letters of abject powerlessness: 'I feel that you are all in conspiracy against me, you are all sneering at me, laughing at me because I don't quite measure up to the accepted normal; I am a nuisance wherever I go and have to be got rid of; it would be a kindly act if I killed myself . . .'

And yet in supplying us with these hectic, funny, painful, lived words, the biographer is in danger of seeming wooden by contrast. Janet Malcolm, writing about the Bloomsbury industry, has suggested that the information of a biography, once removed from its living context, becomes bloodless. 'The canniest biographers, aware of the problem, rush massive transfusions of quotation to the scene.' King has a practised bedside manner but one can experience his own prose as a kind of anaesthetic:

> The pleasure of Janet Frame's first visit to Paris was heightened by her knowledge of French history and culture, a legacy of a good education at Waitaki Girls' High School.

> It did indeed seem that Frame's view of life and her writing style were forged by a deeply internalised tension that grew from a preoccupation with death.

Biography can 'do' letters but it cannot, without extreme violence to the form, do dialogue. Frame's perfect rendering, in The Envoy from Mirror City, of the conversation she has with the hostel receptionist when she first arrives in London ('I'm Janet Frame from New Zealand . . . I'm all the way from New Zealand. I'm just off the boat.') can find no echo for its comedy and pain in King's summary: '. . . all travellers, at some point, have to face an unravelling of arrangements as a result of letters gone astray, bookings doubled up or unannounced changes of schedule.' King here sounds rather like the woman with whom Frame pleads through her tears—a commentator of utter and dismal commonsense. There, there, he seems to say; now grow up.

He then quotes at length from a rather extraordinary passage in the autobiography that follows immediately on from the comic pleading and tears and humiliation:

> I felt fleetingly at the back of my mind the perennial drama of the Arrival and its place in myth and fiction, and I again experienced the thrilling sense of being myself excavated as reality, the ore of the polished fiction. The journey, the arrival, the surprises and problems of arrival . . . For a moment the loss of the letter . . . seemed to be unimportant beside the fictional gift of the loss, as if within every event lay a reflection reached only through the imagination and its various servant languages, as if, like the shadows in Plato's cave, our lives and the world contain mirror cities revealed to us by our imagination, the Envoy.

King hazily connects this with the 'revelation' Frame had following her sister Myrtle's death—'that "real" lives, and the world of dreams and mythology and literature, were intimately connected; and that the individual human imagination was the envoy that moved between those worlds.'

But what is the nature of this 'connection'? Frame's passage begins with an apparent commonplace—the writer consoling herself that this humiliation is raw material for her fiction. However, it is not only 'ore' awaiting the polish of language; the experience is archetypal, that is, already written. Things are simultaneously new and old, ours and the world's. Frame's letter is also, in a section King omits in his quotation, the Letter—the capitalised forebear, begetter of all letters: 'the missing letter, the discovered letter, the letter of such portent that lives are lost and destinies changed as in Macbeth's "They met me in the day of success, and I have learned by the perfectest report, they have more in them than mortal knowledge . . ." and the role of the bearer of the letter, of the successful or failed messenger.'

The consolation then is not that Frame can use what happens to her but that what happens to her has a universal dimension. Frame's narrators are in regular contact with the mythic patterns of their experiences; it is often the way they collapse the newness and strangeness of life into the ready-made, the manageable. When Istina Mavet, in *Faces in the Water*, comes home after five years in hospital, she cannot remember the people she meets on the street and must learn to talk to them 'without knowing who they were'. From this disturbing failure she yet wrests a kind of advantage in that she can choose to see her situation, however ironically, in the grandest cultural terms. 'How could I help a little self-dramatisation around one of the themes of living that is so consistently involved with man's mythology and religion—The Return?'

From this point it is perhaps not difficult to account for the sense we have in her fiction—and which readers may well recoil from—of the particularity of her characters' lives flooded by abstractions; of talk turning rapidly to speech, of scene seguing into emblem, of situation pressed quickly into symbol, of prose changing into poetry. It is not modish or affected but compulsive—not so much a matter of technique as of belief.

Here is a passage from near the beginning of *Faces in the Water*, a book from which it is hard to recover:

> My room stank with sanitary napkins. I did not know where to put them therefore I laid them in the drawer of the landlady's walnut dressing table, in the top drawer, the middle drawer and the bottom drawer; everywhere was the stench of dried blood, of stale foods thrown from the shelves of an internal house that was without tenants or furniture or hope of future lease.

We understand the sanitary napkins but 'an internal house' is of a different order. In mid-sentence, the prose changes the rules without telling us that this is what is happening. The

visceral knocks heads with the virtual in nearly every Frame paragraph.

Frame's novels are not about searches. In the sense of characters seeking a place in the world, the fiction lacks any real interest in describing an arc or trajectory. This is one reason why the stock jargon of book reviewing, with its reliance on the vocabulary of 'development' and 'change', quickly runs out of things to say about Frame's work, taking refuge often in vague utterances about 'beautiful writing'. One enters a Frame novel knowing people have been assigned their place. They have been called 'mad' or 'defective' or 'sick'; or they have been called 'healthy', 'successful', and 'normal'. The 'point' of the novel is to demonstrate, then, a massive failure of imagination. The books are dramas of incorrect assignation. Their sensitivities are to bureaucracy, to organisational manias. They are lock-ups.

As a reader, one seldom feels free inside these works but usually directed, pressured, bullied even. Frame kills off characters without compunction. We cannot with confidence 'follow' anyone through a novel because they are likely to be removed without prior notice. Here is the opening of Chapter 19 of *Living in the Maniototo*:

> When I had been living in the Garretts' house for only a week there was a severe earthquake in northern Italy, and, as one does with distant disasters, I wondered if anyone I knew had been hurt, and I thought of the Garretts, who'd be there now, in the north. Also, as one does, I imagined their dying, and the news coming, and what I should do.
> Two days later the news did come. Irving and Trinity Garrett had died at the opera. They were

31

attending the opera and were buried with the rest of the audience among musical instruments and half-sung arias that became, no doubt, the "steaming lamentations" that rose home into the harmonious blue of the Italian sky, resolving, completing the harmony of many lives.

The Garretts, we understand, are no more than cannon fodder in the war Frame carries on with literary realism. ('I found myself believing the news of their death simply because it was a coincidence that fiction would never have allowed.') Indeed her novels are full of such sacrifices and sudden exits, and yet the tendency, the warring, is not only literary. One doesn't have to rummage deep in the biographical closet to find the original garment of which these writerly dress-ups are the copies. The deaths of two of her sisters by drowning have the same absurd, pointless, wasteful cast as the long line of Frame's fictional deaths, though none attain the heights either of pained ridiculousness (the 'new' arm Myrtle is given when extracted from the family photograph) or vivid desolation (Isabel's lead coffin emerging from the train; Frame's mother's hair changing from brown-grey to white) that illuminate those events and give them such frightening force.

Just as we remember Myrtle's fake arm but not Myrtle, we remember vividly no one from Frame's fiction but we may recall certain tangles her people get into, certain pressing ironies—Dr Talbot Edelman, the Death Studies expert in *Daughter Buffalo*, packing his dead dog in a suitcase; Erlene in *Scented Gardens for the Blind*, who has lost the power of speech, wishing her mother would stop talking. Frame is really a creator of predicament, not character. Her people do not chance upon their crises but dwell in them so completely, so suffocatingly, that it is others, free of such burdens, who appear less than human. The giveaway is always language. Revisiting her sisters' deaths in *Daughter Buffalo*, Frame has her narrator observe their new status as bereft siblings: 'We acquired the prestige of being in a family where someone had "died young", a "blossom plucked before her time", a life full of promise "cut off tragically".' Dementedly social, routinely inane, the speakers of such phrases lack the insight to be afflicted.

Likewise, Frame's interest in novels within novels—reaching its height in the later works, *Living in the Maniototo* and *The Carpathians*—which might tempt us in the direction of postmodernist manners, seems to me to have instead, at its heart, two less modish impulses. First, a deep-seated suspicion of all acts of consolation—the conventional novel, victimised by notions of progress and improvement, tells us what we want to hear; namely, that if we work hard at it, we can escape our situation. The second impulse derives from that famously, personally acquired feel for institutional imposition, for regimentation that is arbitrary. The story, the book, is an institution; the teller, a sort of wilful authority with executive powers. Another predicament, another lock-up.

Of course, such a reading relies without much subtlety on the biographical data, on a knowledge of the former psychiatric patient compelled to relive her years within institutions. And maybe we'd look somewhere else for a template if the letters didn't confirm the impression that Frame herself was constantly drawn to make this comparison. The YMCA in London, and almost ten years later the flat she first occupies as Burns Fellow, are near-facsimiles of mental hospitals—'but with a key, and without the horror'; even Yaddo second time around feels too institutional: 'I haven't laughed—real laughter—for ages and ages . . . [Everyone] is determined not to spill a clue of irrationality or disorder, and one is reminded all the time that one is a Writer, and Artist.'

It's important to register the temperature of these pronouncements. When Frame says to her friends that Yaddo is the sort of institution that she can't tolerate—'a concentration camp where one could neither concentrate nor camp'—it is not that she is joking exactly nor, as King unnecessarily puts it, 'writing with a degree of exaggeration'; but it is certainly a distinctive sort of witticism and through it she is proving her health, the soundness of her mind, its sense of proportion—*she* can laugh even if others can't or won't. It is the characteristic turn of her prose to take in humorously the calamity of her life and spit it back as linguistic playfulness.

The soundness of her mind was of course something in which Frame had more than a passing linguistic interest.

Writing, she says in the autobiography, saves her life, but we know from King's biography that it does not 'cure' her life. The distinction is worth making since the tendency is to view the triumph as more or less complete with the narrow escape from a leucotomy following the news that her first book had won a literary prize. The drama is vivid and terrifying no matter how often it is played out. And while it would take a hard heart not to find the confluence of these forces almost overwhelming—literature versus the scalpel, the indelible inscription of a sensibility against its irreversible removal—it was only the beginning. That was 1952. One of this biography's most useful services is to place before us, with sensitivity, the record of Frame's admissions to hospitals. Frame would continue to receive psychiatric care, on and off, for years after her initial release from Seacliff, often admitting herself and gaining manifest benefits from her treatment. Psychiatry was destructive but also useful.

The biography, since it cannot pay the writing much attention, barely underlines something that the autobiography makes clear, namely that Frame's own personal predicament was not only the engine of her fiction but that this fiction conveyed a single passenger: Janet Frame was Janet Frame's sole fare. On account of her intelligence and linguistic resourcefulness and strength, she collected again and again from this traveller; but the sense that it is the same coin changing hands is a considerable one. When she came to name herself as herself, something mysterious and moving happened. The autobiography is the glorious work everyone says it is because it reveals the first great character of Frame's writing and, at the risk of sounding back-handed, a subject that truly matches her mind. In the ways the autobiography details the first thirty or so years, we do not feel the machinery of a theme but rather the chanciness of a life. It tells of a prisoner but it feels like a liberation.

Here the prodigiousness of her memory appears as the storehouse of her fiction. That memory—for songs, for poems, for things, for sayings, for sensations—is also, I think, the kind of structure which the writer has difficulty seeing around. Like any grand edifice, it provides the view but it obstructs the view. Which is probably another way of making the rather trite observation that despite her many moves, her many houses, Frame is always somehow stuck in Oamaru; stuck with that brother, stuck with that hair. This is always the case, whether we are writers or not. Our lives are gifts as well as curses. We are healthy *and* sick, sensitive and callous, sane and mad, or better to say, we live on the scale that connects these points. Like the bubble in a spirit level, we need only travel a short distance to indicate a massive reorientation. Of course, Frame knows this, and yet the predetermined antagonisms of her fiction have seldom allowed much play along the scale. In the autobiography, however, that sense of confinement is out the window.

Our sympathy is won not by the 'terrible life' Frame has endured—or not most lastingly by that—but by her astonishing readmission into that life. Only *Faces in the Water* has a comparable power. She collapses the distance between then and now so utterly, so freely, so lovingly. Majestically, she allows herself failure, uncertainty, dishonesty—she is a victim not simply of others but of herself, her bad choices and failures of nerve, and she lets us see how others suffer because of her. Most importantly, she does not always enlist us on her side—or not obviously at least. There is no bullying going on.

What are we to make, for instance, of this observation? Frame is remembering her dislike of the woman in the bed next to her, whom she calls 'repulsive': 'I wonder now about the treatment of psychiatric and other patients, who release as it were a chemical, an invitation to be disliked and who therefore have to fight (inducing further dislike and antagonism) for sympathy and fairness.'

The autobiography is also a riveting portrait of shyness or of the resourcefulness of timidity. One example might show us the worth of this: Frame's invention of a serial story while teaching to avoid being 'caught out' by the headmaster and her retreat to her room to avoid the staffroom. The candour lets us understand that timidity is not a nothing but an intense and exhausting activity requiring foresight, organisation, determination. Timid people are often startlingly prepared for human engagement—much of their behaviour is not a negation of a hostile world but a rehearsal for an unlikely triumph in that world. The timid are always getting ready. And the way a young woman's supposed passivity is always falling away under close examination of the facts shouldn't surprise us but it does.

The biography carries on this work of curing our complacency. The Janet Frame who can take apart a motorbike and put it back together again is a valuable addition to our other Frames.

There is yet another Frame in the life story, though she does not bear her name. She is a sort of eerie double and she inhabits the fiction at all its most vulnerable points. Nola, who undergoes the leucotomy Frame was scheduled for, is a haunting figure for the reader but for Frame she is a binding one. Frame keeps in touch with 'dehumanised' Nola 'and it was like living in a fairytale where conscience, and what might have been, and what was, not only speak but spring to life and become a living companion, a reminder.'

The discomforting question which sits

somewhere behind the autobiography and has to do with the ultimate dispensation granted to characters in any Frame novel is perhaps best approached through this figure, this reminder. Why does Frame deny to her characters the success she herself has had? Her own life story is, after all, in its simplest terms, one of high achievement and obstacles overcome. The reasons might plausibly be connected to a common enough proposition: survivor's guilt. There is no extension of optimism because Frame feels she's been lucky; because it could have been her under the knife, because her work therefore stands on something accidental, contingent, fluky. Under this rubric, fate's capriciousness in her life becomes in her novels a kind of designed malice—the horrors are nearly always institutionalised, programmed, irresistible. They are marked like this as a matter of loyalty to the real people Frame knew who suffered. And they are articulated in the sinister, bureaucratic voice of characters such as the Prime Minister in *Intensive Care* who urges citizens, 'Think not of the human race in the abstract, think of people you know who have struggled for years under the handicap of being human and who would be eased of their distressing life by this new legislation.' The legislation involves an operation on the brain.

It is Nola who stands behind the final paragraphs of *Faces in the Water*, in which her fellow patient delivers the most beautiful ending in our literature:

> I looked away from them and tried not to think of them and repeated to myself what one of the nurses had told me, "when you leave hospital you must forget all you have ever seen, put it out of your mind completely as if it never happened, and go and live a normal life in the outside world."
> And by what I have written in this document you will see, won't you, that I have obeyed her?

If exercising over the title of a book moves probably the weakest muscle in the reviewer's body, there remains a twitch. *Wrestling*. King is defiantly not a wrestling writer. His narrative is disconcertingly smooth. He is a brilliant organiser but there is always the sense that by the time the words are hitting the page, his subject has hit the deck. How could it be otherwise? What would a biography look like if it didn't suggest, above all, immense composure and certainty? It would look, of course, like fiction.

There is a moment at the end of the biography when King makes a gesture towards something like this sort of unknowability. He provides a vignette of himself and his subject as she tells her life 'in a tone that acknowledged past tragedies but seemed more frequently to tremble on the brink of laughter.'

> Talking *and* writing, she conveyed a vivid sense that reality itself is a fiction, and one's grasp on it no more than preposterous pretence and pretension. And that sense delights her, as it does her readers and listener.

A cosy scene, and perhaps harmlessly insincere on both sides. King has written enough decent history to know that reality is rather unlike fiction to those suffering it, and Frame would hardly have bothered to circulate to prying professors the Cawley letter stating that her affliction was 'unhappiness' and not mental illness if she had had this sort of equanimity about error. For both these writers there are category mistakes whose correction is not just a matter of principle but of survival. Yet King is drawn to the scene. It feels like the sort of thing a writer says, and that a biographer might subscribe to in that moment when the book is done and a little humility is in order. In fact, except for this moment, the book he's written is without pretension or pretence.

This urge to feel 'delight', arriving as it does so late in the day, alerts us to the biographer's anxiety. It is as if King has just noticed the room temperature of his work and seeks now a little heat. Yet biography of this sort is a kind of drill, a procedure—and then this, and then this. This is why as a form it rarely moves us as fiction does and as autobiography can. Its finger cannot be pricked by what Frame calls 'the bent hairpin of unreason'. And as readers we conspire with the form, shrinking its impact. When biography wants to be suggestive, we read it as only coy. When it wants the evidence to speak for itself, we feel it is being evasive. When it aims for the poetic—as in the Prologue—we squirm in our seats. We allow it none of the sins for which more 'creative' forms are forgiven and indeed cherished. It is an institution and we require it to be—as Frame requires her institutions to be—predictable and imaginatively deficient though with terrible powers. Biography, we see, is itself a sort of lock-up.

ANDREW JOHNSTON

As, When, While

for Rosalind Dilys

Like switches or bridges, engines, hinges,
doors from now to now,

the words themselves are patient,
they're here for the duration.

'As', for instance, swings like
the door of a saloon

a cowboy just stepped through,
something on his mind—

an alibi, a lullaby, a syllable
he carries from room to room.

★

He was taking his time when the time came
to step through a word and

into our conversation, as if to say,
why go when you can

stand in the doorway talking—
the door the one marked 'When'

we have a habit of leaving open—
holding everyone up and holding up

the world. When you say the word
a cup, half-full, is still filling.

          ⋆

While we were talking in the house of words
a wind turned the pages we'd written:

imagine six billion breathing, imagine
every human thing happening. If

the words could speak they'd say,
Relax—this is the present,

it's a big house, everyone
in the world is coming and going,

through doors marked
As, When, While.

ROGER McDONALD

Wild Man in Landscape

I see the fettlers' train snaking through the sandhills. The iron tracks straighten and the train gathers speed, entrancing a man who hangs from the rattling window frame going farther with each jump of the rails into his dream of Australia, with a sense of always returning.

He can't let go adjectives from his mind: the red-purpled land, the blood-deep desert, the red-fire beetles winking from the firebox as day goes down and the train goes racing for the dark mountains across the desert floor.

Bearded figures, Italian prisoners of war, stand up from the rails and get out of the way. Ranked beside the train they call out greetings. The man leans out shouting, *Come sta!* And the blurred faces call back *Bene! Bene!* And he looks back at them receding, filled with emotion at their shared exile and the way the desert receives them.

He leaves the railway camp making emotional farewells to the boozers and brawlers sharing his loneliness—getting away early in cold starlight, out to the road which recedes in perspective, and where the looped wires of the overland telegraph line are highlighted before the burnt-red coming day. His heart is raked by the cry of black cockatoos. He longs for words of barbarous beauty equivalent to the bird calls. A tall, strong-shouldered man with a mop of Shelleyan hair, eyes rolling like a confused stallion's, with a swaying gait, he was trained to the saddle in stock camps since boyhood and in boyhood was taken by the ringers in those camps and thrown on a blanket and raped.

Far north, he wakes in a shack on the banks of the Roper River, props himself on an elbow and lets morning light fill his head through gaps in the walls. Flame of blossom strikes him, crimson flowers of mistletoe falling like a woman's hair—but he asks, was ever a woman as beautiful as this gum, standing with smooth white limbs against the pure opal sky?

At night the tree is a dark cloud and he listens to cicadas drumming. She is the girl of a scattered tribe, the dark cloud holding a secret of the land. She is one of the people he sees, and humbly bows to, his mortal vision so intense it would drag him into another state of being if he wasn't a human being and thus held like a spirit in a rock.

They are tall, long-haired visitors in their country standing off and holding spears. He sees them from the windows of the workers' train; sees them in a wrecked homestead where they providentially find shelter from the wind—their campfire burning like a star at rest among ruins of the fallen stone. He wants to find his own country as they do when they come in and spread their mission blankets on the ground beneath the dark acacia and bauhinia trees, surrounded by children and dogs, carrying dilly-bags and bundles of possessions tied up in strips of some old coloured dress. He wants, and he longs, and he craves: but he cannot have what they have in smouldering ash and fume behind the trees, because the thin-grassed ridges of their land are their home wherever they camp, but can be his only in passing passion.

By the riverbank and around the lagoon his words are leaves from the paperbark trees falling on water. Words are his join between what is not, and what can never be. When sunlight enters his shack in the morning it casts across his bed the pattern of fig and palm leaves. The sun, he says, won't grant him rest. His feelings tempt by becoming half-mythological, appearing in recurrent shapes—birds, shadows, stars, fires, trees—exciting him and wrenching him into love which is always heightened, and gaining him a certain celebrity and notoriety when he comes down to Adelaide like a wild man, a snorting primitive, one who has got there before the rest. But never mind that.

As yet unapproachable hills rise out of the dawn. Anthills stand ever away in the scrub and dry grass. Brumbies come out of the purple ranges and feed in the reeds of the billabong where Birwain mourned Nerida, dived in and was changed to reeds. Would that he could be changed to reeds and spears of reeds, he roars, that fringe the lilies opening far out among their floating leaves!

Everything he witnesses has a moment of perfection, the tea-tree petals slipping into his billycan as he dips, and say for example a wondrous commingling of birdsong at dawn and the vague forms of trees filling the opening of his tent. One bird keeps singing, the rain of the rest ceases and the one voice of all sings purely on, but sings in ending. This never happens again, though he camps in the same place—everything happens with such perfection and then is celebrated and then mourned. His verbs pierce, his nouns hammer, his adverbs splash the brow, his adjectives pour their red, vermilion, and their crimson flush. Look where it takes him. All comes down to boots and shirts and hat flung on the floor, telling their tale of jobs, unrest and change.

But he makes a prayer: Morning so beautiful that the breathing trees spread their boughs against the moving sea in adoration.

Then he is back in the siding-shed transfixed by stars, and the train comes with its blinding light: Nailed boots to disturb his meditation. Into the day with the birds talking into his ears he goes, curlew, wagtail, lorikeet, thrush and wren his outriders.

But mostly it's the budgerigars, those small parrots no bigger than a newborn baby's fist that he follows, hundreds to a flock, thousands, tens of thousands and then millions darkening the sky. They capture and mirror the torments of his mind, the unfinished and unseeking self-taught brain so elegiac and overactive. They come in a flash, particled, as he sees them, throated with a shrill fierce cry, writhing and deployed in banners of birdsmoke and streaming into the grey mulga scrub and then soaring as if from a blaze of fire. They come into the trees at Deep Well, into the trees he calls spirit-trees alive with birds clustering them—Deep Well where the fettlers' car travelled towards the cool blue rising wave that was the Ooraminna Range, where, choosing to be a fettler, he worked to lay red gum sleepers, lined and spiked the rails with adze and hammer, shovel and bar.

He was past sixty the time I met him. I was in my twenties. He was the poet, leonine, sitting with his big white dog and saying nothing; fidgety, self-conscious, bursting with ego and feigning indifference. I could see it in the way he breathed, held himself, and almost snorted with self-willed invisibility and frightened me with his self-importance.

I had heard he was foolish and made difficulties, lived in his feelings too much, exploded. But when I spoke to him he stood and opened his hands with ease and acceptance, slouched a little into the story-telling mode of the country as I struggled to say what his writing meant to me. I started reciting 'Deep Well', lines where the spirit trees writhed in cool white limbs and budgerigar, and it fell away into a mumble, I got the words wrong—but did it matter? As I spoke my praise he opened like a desert flower and uncrinkled a thousand curious petals.

'Wild Man in Landscape' is based on the poetry of Roland Robinson (1912–92). Many of the words and phrases used are taken from three books of his poetry, *Language of Sand* (1949), *Tumult of the Swans* (1953), and *Deep Well* (1962). I am also indebted to *The Drift of Things* (1972), the first volume of his autobiography. —RM

JEFFREY PAPAROA HOLMAN

The iconography of birds

(for Les Murray)

Christ the Pelican tears His own
breast in the rose window of heaven.

Across the Gothic vault of the sky
migrate the wings of faith, as waders fly

the jam-packed estuary, each knot,
oystercatcher, bar-tailed godwit

feathered with the flag of Odysseus,
wings oar-dipping from parenthesis

to parenthesis of the food season's
cornucopian twin hemispheres.

Christ the Dove migrates there with them
as herds of dwindling crosses vote for a heaven

they can't see, can't touch, can't taste or smell
but know is there by scriptures from the gene pool

drummed into hearts by the wingbeat:
instinct, instinct, instinct, instinct.

no ifs or buts about it

(for my father and his creed)

You never told me what you did believe.
We found it in your wallet, with the RSA
Member's Card for 1970. It was cyclostyled
in methylated purple on the back of Naval
Message sheet S1320e, Revised December 1931.
It was faded, folded, tatty, your broken heart.
It was Kipling's 'IF', your battle flag and creed.
It's all mine now, complete with barking demons:
'If!' they howl at me, 'If! If!'
'Get in behind!' I snap, 'Get in behind!'

★

I'm flying over the River If
in a flimsy Fairey Fruitbat:
banking left through wires
I see that *old Moulmein*
Pagoda, boys, but ah, she's
gone, *me Burmah Gal*, we
loved to call Myanmar Sal
with *her whackin white cheroot*
and that there *heathen idol's*
Golden Boot she kissed
but never me, and now she's
under house arrest for saying
'No more Junta!' I'm banking
right now, boys, where the If
flows into the mighty Ever
and I tell you, she's a beauty . . . !
She's a golden, golden river
skirting domes.

44

*

If you'd told me what I wanted
to know, I wouldn't have to do

what I do, making a lifetime up.
We could have sailed in claddy

wood boats, outriggers spliced
with flax, bobbling over tiny

rapids in ditches coming home
from school. You could pluck

parrots out of nowhere and tell
me the secret words for *Dragonlair*.

Yes you could. You were my giant, you
sailed to the edge of the world and

if you still would, we could do all this
together, and I won't call you IF

anymore, you'll be my *Heromaster*
and I'll be *Davey Jones*, your Chief.

DAVID GLYNN

Drownland
(Extract from a work in progress)

Beneath the surface of the lake there is a town, only no one lives there
any more.

Approaching it from the east you find yourself in a shallow river, frigid
with snow-melt, barely flowing, that snakes over a gravel bed between
boulders the size of cars, until eventually, as you swim upstream, you come to
the dam. At the bottom of the spillway, looking up, you see grey concrete slick
as glass, almost vertical between two huge angled buttresses rising up higher
than you could ever imagine, impassable.

There is another way. The feeder pipes rise at a shallower angle, up
through the dam's dark heart. The turbines have been stilled, and you pass
between the blades and ascend slowly through a vast black silent steel shaft
until, hundreds of feet higher now, you emerge into the grey-green world of
the lake.

You wait, letting your eyes adjust from darkness to the murky half-light,
and then you dive.

For miles along the valley floor lie what used to be orchards, row on row of
cherry and peach and apricot trees whose decaying limbs do not even wave
but simply stretch, skeletal, towards a sky that they will never see again.
Occasionally a farmhouse drifts by below you, blind-eyed, staring into
nothing. You are following the old road: you could follow it with your eyes
closed, so familiar is it, straight as a die seven miles up the valley, and everything on either side of it drowned, covered in a loose layer of silt that stirs
lightly as you pass. There is no sound. There are no ghosts.

And then you come to a sign, for the benefit of anyone who might still
attempt to drive this road. *Welcome to* ——, it reads.

Some welcome.

You wonder for a moment why everything is coloured the same dull aqueous green until you remember that you are underwater, and then you wonder how it is that you can breathe. Not that it matters. You are at the edge of town now.

Everything is so familiar that it has become strange, like a word on a page looked at too long. Streets and houses from your childhood, shops and playgrounds and telephone poles and mailboxes and . . .

There is your house.

It squats at the end of the cul-de-sac where round and round and round you used to ride, until you were old enough to escape to the valley beyond. The empty street, the pregnant silence, a sense of expectancy. You are waiting for someone. You hang suspended for longer than you can count.

Until you realise who it is you are waiting for.

Yourself.

Expecting him to appear on that old, red, too-large bicycle, a small boy riding the streets of a deserted town, crying out the names of those who used to live there. And the longer you wait, the more sure you are that he will come.

But you are floating upwards, streets and houses receding into the murk, even though you know he is there, alone, and that he needs you. The light above you gets brighter as you draw close to the surface, while below you the town is no more than a dark smudge at the bottom of a lake. Even so, you can still see him in your mind's eye, a boy who is you and not you, riding, calling. But you cannot hear his cry now, only a rushing in your ears as you are swept upwards, and as you break the surface you realise that all this time you have been holding your breath, and your body explodes from the water into golden sunlight and you open your mouth and suck all the air you can into the void that is your chest, gasping, choking, while on the banks of the lake the new town that they built there goes on about its business under a brittle morning sun, paying you no mind.

Your name is Luther, and this is your dream.

Luther. A pause. Luther—. Someone was prodding him. He opened his eyes. He could see his feet. Floating between them were four empty beer bottles, bobbing in the cloudy water of a bath that had cooled to the temperature of blood.

'What?' he said.

'It's four o'clock.'

'So?'

'You said you were going to open at five.'

'It's only four.'

'Jesus.'

The only reason to open the doors of a bar is that there are people who want to drink, and he suspected that none of his customers had quite readied themselves for more. Yet. As much as anything else, serious drinkers can be defined by their internal clock. There are morning drinkers, who must be drunk by midday. There are afternoon drinkers, whose need becomes greater the closer they get to those terrible rituals that play out at the end of the day; dinner, television, bed. And then there are evening drinkers, drunk by nine but able, once they have again accepted their ever-recurring fate, to remain drunk until four or five or nine the following day. Luther's best customers were of the latter kind, and an hour either way made little difference to them.

So he took his time. He ran one hand over cheek and jawbone, debating whether to shave. Through the open window he could hear the city rise sluggishly to its knees as it prepared to crawl home to the suburbs. No, he decided, the night could have him as he was. He pulled the plug, rose, walked away wetly from the sound of empty bottles clinking against enamel as the plughole's tiny vortex whirled them round.

Rain drummed softly on the roof as he dressed. He pulled on his boots. In the kitchen the words IM GONE were spelled out on the fridge door in a child's brightly coloured magnetic plastic letters, just in case he had not noticed her absence. Good for you, he thought, and opened the fridge for another beer, with the feeling even as he raised it that it might not assuage his thirst.

Luther rarely remembered his dreams—it was reality that put him out of sorts, the more prosaic details of unmopped floors and unwashed glasses. That, and the knowledge that he would not quell the desire that burned his flesh and froze in his bones if he drowned it in an ocean of beer, or a river of bourbon. It was an irony of some beauty: him, owning a bar, someone for whom drunkenness just would not suffice.

He had taken it—in exchange for their debt—off the hands of two brothers who, blind with the optimism of youth, had not realised that the rule about location applies to everybody, or that naming a business venture after Kurtz was probably not a good idea. And now it was his, a decrepit building on a moribund street at the edge of the city.

Still, even Pound had his cage, he thought, descending the stairs, throwing open the door and walking out, boot-heels ringing on the wooden floor, into the middle of the cavernous space that was his prison, his domain.

It was spacious, for a cell. It had started life as a grain store, the two doors at the back still opening directly over the lane, though in the succeeding decades its bricks had seen all manner of enterprise come and go. The ceiling rose to its apex thirty feet above the floorboards, and over the back half had been built the mezzanine in which Luther now lived. At the front a set of stairs up which you could drive a bus led down to the street. Behind the stairs lay the ground floor. That was storage, piled high with the detritus of a century's endeavour, rolls of carpet, old lathes without motors, the gutted carcass of a '38 Ford, hanks of rope and electrical flex and box upon box of things too useless to throw away. Hours he had spent down here. It was his favourite place, save for the roof. Steeply pitched, clad in corrugated iron, accessible by a trapdoor set into its northern slope, the roof that in midsummer became too hot to walk on even with shoes, though as the shadows lengthened you might climb it, carrying a folded blanket and a book, and let it raise you above the city that shimmered below, blue and green and gold, fragile as a mirage.

It was after five, the light failing by degrees. He descended the stairs, unbolted the doors and pushed them open. 'Greetings, gentlemen,' he said with a flourish. A man in a suit glanced sideways as he strode past, but that was all.

Never mind. For Luther, there was no finer hour than twilight in autumn. Especially when it rained. The magic hour between five and six when, if you turned no light on, you could actually see the darkness deepen incrementally, watch the red glow bleed from an endless stream of tail lights and spill over the rain-soaked streets, mixing with the oil and the neon to make a palette with which you could paint almost anything, so long as it was loneliness, loss or freedom. Luther loved the smell, the sound, the motion. He loved the way that even the pedestrians who bustled past him, head down, shoulders hunched, paid him no mind.

He walked to the kerb. It was like standing on the bank of a quickly flow-ing river. As the cars streamed by each occupant flashed briefly in silhouette. Where were they going? Could all of them be going home to the houses that glowed gold in his imagination? It seemed to him that they must, for surely no one could move so intently toward an emptiness not of their own choos-ing.

Rain drummed heavier now on the awning above his head, and he recalled a rhyme. *The rain it raineth on the just, and on the unjust fella. But it raineth more upon the just, for the unjust stole the just's umbrella.* Or something like that. All about him, on the pavement and the street, people scurried home unpro-tected from the sudden rain. He smiled. Which of you is just, he asked himself, turning away from the ceaseless flow, and which truly deserves the umbrella?

Tsunami Memories:
Disaster-Tourism on the Big Island
Mike Davis

HILO, ACCORDING to that indefatigable Victorian globetrotter, Isabella Bird Bishop (*Six Months in the Sandwich Islands*), 'is the paradise of Hawai'i. What Honolulu attempts to be, Hilo is without effort.' Some of the lotus-eating ambience, to be sure, has eroded from the capital of the Big Island since portly Isabella was rowed ashore in 1875. With the construction of the modern breakwater, few 'athletes, like the bronzes of the Naples Museum, ride the waves on their surf-boards', and the morning commute, complete with mini-gridlock on Highway 11, has replaced the 'brilliant dressed riders' in their mu'u-mu'us and leis cantering along the beach.

Yet the fundamental things still apply: a greenness that makes Ireland look grey encircling a perfect crescent bay with Pele's immense thrones, Mauna Loa and snow-capped Mauna Kea, piercing the cloudbank in the background. Unlike balmy but deeply troubled Honolulu, which debates whether it is metamorphosing into Orange County or Las Vegas, soggy Hilo (ten feet of annual rain-fall—a formidable deterrent to gentrification) retains a homespun Hawaiian character. Culturally it is an 'ohana (extended family) not a malihini (stranger's) town, and, despite the recent eruption of a regional mall (Prince Kuhio Plaza) and a handful of sub-Waikiki hotel towers, it is still possible to agree with Bishop that this city of 45,000 just below the Tropic of Cancer is 'clothed in poetry'.

Yet Hilo's broad grin also displays some missing teeth. The city has warily retreated from its waterfront. The scores of cafés, cheap hotels, and warehouses, as well as the famed Hilo Theater, that once lined the bay side of Kamehameha Avenue downtown are now a parking strip. Further south the shoreline neighbourhood of Shinmachi ('new town') has become Mooheau Park, while all that remains of boisterous Waiakea Town (or Yashijima) on the Wailoa River is the Social Settlement clock tower, its hands forever frozen at 1.04 a.m. An important part of Hilo past—the very heart of its Japanese working-class tradition—has disappeared.

1. The Tsunami Museum

Hilo's parks and open spaces gracefully dissimulate a tragic history. No inhabited landscape in the United States (or colonised Polynesia, if you prefer) is so regularly convulsed by extreme natural forces. If Mauna Loa's lavas have repeatedly threatened the city but at the last minute miraculously spared it (thanks to native Hawaiian prayer or Army Air Corps bombs), the Pacific has been crueller. As the windward flank of the Hawaiian archipelago, Hilo and the adjacent Hamakua Coast are the bull's-eye for tidal waves originating from earthquakes anywhere in a vast arc from Kamchatka to Tierra del Fuego.

Twice since World War Two, mountainous tsunamis have surged over the breakwater. The 'April Fools' 1946 waves devastated Shinmachi and downtown (fifty-seven dead), as well as inundating the school at Laupahoehoe Point, twenty-six miles north of Hilo, and drowning twenty-four teachers and students. Another sixty-one people perished in the early morning of May 22, 1960, when an even bigger tsunami hit downtown with such force that all the parking meters along Kamehameha Avenue were bent to the

Images courtesy Mike Davis.

ground. The Waiakea district with its famous
fish market and sampan landing, largely
spared in 1946, was virtually obliterated.

To mitigate future destruction, the bay
front was redeveloped into a green-belt buffer
zone, which, in addition to the famous
Waiakea clock, includes a memorial plaza
dedicated to the Shinmachi victims of 1946.
Beyond this swelling wall of black lava, meant
to suggest the lethal beauty of a tsunami, the
Army Corps of Engineers constructed a large
landfill plateau safely above the 1960 high-

water mark. As a gesture of confidence, state
and federal offices were relocated here, along
with the aptly named Kaiko'o ('violent seas') Mall.

Tsunamis recently have come to vie with
orchids and hula (the annual 'Merrie Monarch
Festival') as Hilo's principal civic symbol. It is
a populist phenomenon that defies the rule
that cities always repress the memory of
disaster. Tourists, after all, are not invited to
celebrate 'Earthquake Day' in San Francisco or
to tour the 'Terrorism Museum' in Oklahoma
City. Nor did Hilo itself, until the last decade,

53

care much about monumentalising its unique exposure to the combined wraths of nature—volcanoes, earthquakes, tsunamis and hurricanes.

The turning point in 1996 was the coincidence of the fiftieth anniversary of the 1946 tragedy with the 'Last Harvest' on the Big Island's sole remaining sugar plantation at Kaʻu. For more than a century sugar had been the chief livelihood of Hilo and the neighbouring Puna and Hamakua coasts. The region's multi-ethnic popular culture had been shaped by generations of shared toil in the cane fields, as well as by the heroic battle to organise the plantations. (Hawaiʻi, thanks to local activists of the ILWU—the International Longshore & Warehouse Union—became the unique successful instance of high-wage agricultural unionisation in US history.) The death of the island's sugar industry—victim of non-union Florida mills and Midwest corn sweeteners—has been the one disaster from which recovery, so far, has proven impossible.

Economic crisis has in turn given urgency to public memory. The dramatic outpouring of tsunami recollections in 1996, which led to the establishment of the Pacific Tsunami Museum two years later, has been a therapeutic catalyst for a larger dialogue about community survival and intergenerational continuity in the face of a decade-long state and local recession that has forced so many young kamaʻāina (Hawaiian-born) families to emigrate to the mainland. (Hawaiian labour migration to Las Vegas is one of the ten largest interstate population streams in the country, and an estimated 40,000 islanders now live in the Glitterdome.) 'Talking tsunami', moreover, potentially opens the way for the recovery of other, more

controversial, collective memories, including Hilo's militant labour history and the struggle to defend native Hawaiian sovereignty.

Even a casual visitor to the museum, which is housed in a massive art deco bank building on Kamehameha Avenue that withstood the furies of 1946 and 1960, ends up spellbound by the Homeric tales of the survivors who come to 'talk story' and visit friends. (The local newspaper now devotes a regular column to these narratives.) Yet the terrain of memory is complex, and the museum is obviously a coalition of different agendas. It is my outsider's impression—and I apologise for any caricature—that at least four kinds of interests participate in the current memorialisation of tsunami and 'island heritage'.

The 'boosters'—like the character in John Sayles's film Limbo who wants to Disneyfy the Alaskan wilderness—perceive tsunami history as a thrilling adventure-theme to attract more visitor dollars from the tourist-rich (and heavily Californianised) Kona side of the island. The 'dowagers', like their matronly counterparts in other small towns, are concerned to preserve the hegemony of old ruling haole (white) families over anything that smacks of genealogy or local history. The tsunami 'buffs', meanwhile, are simply enthralled by the romance of these spectacular cataclysms.

But the principal constituency of the museum are the 'activists' (although some will disdain such a loaded term) struggling to preserve 'ohana values in the face of the centrifugal forces of deindustrialisation, out-migration, and scattered gentrification. Two groups in particular have become exemplary

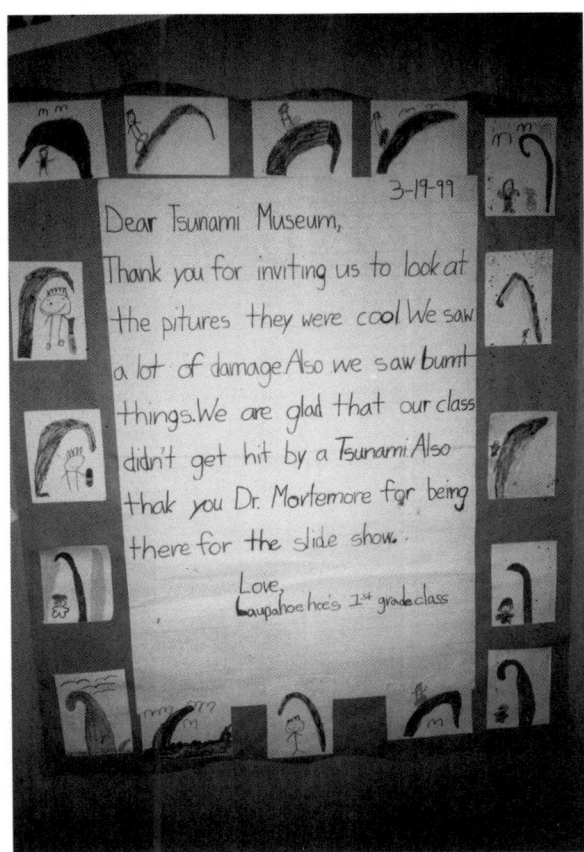

grassroots historians. For both the oldsters of the Waiakea Pirates Athletic Club, custodians of the famous clock, and the youngsters of Laupahoehoe School, curators of an oral history of the 1946 tragedy, tsunamis are a way of evoking solidarity, courage and community identity.

2. The Waiakea Pirates

Although the Hilo region offers a diverse menu of tsunami ruins and monuments (including the Shinmachi memorial, the site of the Hakalau Mill, and the Museum itself), it is the Waiakea Clock that tourists take home as an image on a T-shirt or even as a ten-inch replica. The Clock, saved from the rubble in 1960 and restored to its original location in 1984 by the Waiakea Pirates, was originally erected in 1939 outside the Social Settlement Gym to honour a prominent *haole* planter's wife.

Settlement houses, of course, are usually associated with boweries and back-of-the-yards. And, indeed, from the perspective of the Hawaiian Board of Missions, which established the Social Settlement in 1900 'to make Waiakea a clean, sober, industrious, wholesome and desirable community', this largely Japanese town of five thousand people across from the Hilo Iron Works and next to the Port was an incipient 'slum'. Certainly it had a tough, rambunctious atmosphere and Waiakea kids were famous for Our Gang monikers that would not have been out of place in Hell's Kitchen: 'Spitoon' Hamano, 'Wreck' Matsuno, 'Blackie' Takemura, 'Bones' Kondo, 'Cowboy Joe' Okahara, and so on.

More to the point, however, Waiakea was a source of *haole* anxiety because it was site of the largest concentration of blue-collar workers on the Big Island—mill labourers, sampan fishermen, railroaders and stevedores—and the crucible for trade unionism and radical politics. In 1935 Harry Kamoku, a Chinese-Hawaiian from Waiakea who had picketed with Harry Bridges during the San Francisco General Strike, returned to lead a successful revolt of longshoremen at the Hilo Port. The ILWU hall at 1383 Kamehameha Avenue in Waiakea (now the third hole of the Country Club Hawai'i golf course) became the regional headquarters of the Congress of Industrial Organizations (CIO).

On 1 August 1938 several hundred longshoremen, unionised laundry women and Waiakea residents marched to the wharves in a show of solidarity with the striking CIO sailors of the Inter-Island Steam Navigation Company. As the scab freighter SS *Waialeale* arrived from Honolulu, police and company goons armed with shotguns and bayonets savagely attacked peaceful demonstrators. Nearly a quarter of the crowd, including several children, were wounded in what became notorious as the 'Hilo Massacre'. As an outraged Harry Kamoku reported to the ILWU in Honolulu: 'They shot us down like a herd of sheep. We didn't have a chance. The firing kept up for about five minutes. They just kept on pumping buckshot and bullets into our bodies. They shot men in the back as they ran. They shot men who were trying to help wounded comrades and women. They ripped their bodies with bayonets.' (After the war, Kamoku played a leading role in unionising the sugar plantations on the Hamakua Coast north of Hilo.)

In this troubled era, the only passion that equalled Waiakea's enthusiasm for the labour movement was baseball, and the Depression years were the golden age of Hilo's powerhouse Commercial and Japanese leagues. Founded in 1924 as the first club open to all ethnic groups, the Waiakea Pirates quickly became the Brooklyn Dodgers of island baseball. The big-league calibre of play at Honolulu Park was famously demonstrated in 1933 when a *haole* player from the mainland went to bat against the legendary Pirates' pitcher Taffy Okamura. After repeatedly striking Babe Ruth out, Okamura was obliged to slow down his fast ball so that the visitor could hit it.

In the post-war years, as the ILWU was winning strikes and organising sugar workers into a powerful union, the Pirates maintained their pre-eminence in the new 100th Battalion Memorial Baseball League: dedicated to the celebrated Nisei combat unit in which so many Waiakea men had served. Both the 1960

rvesting Sugar Cane

baseball season and the sugar harvest were in full swing when the 'earthquake of the century' devastated the southern coast of Chile on 22 May.

It took fifteen hours for the quake's energy to cross the Pacific. The warning sirens installed after 1946 began wailing at 8.30 that evening, but reassuring reports from Tahiti of waves barely three feet high induced a false sense of security. The Waiakea sampan fleet sought safety in the open ocean, but dare-devil youngsters gathered at the Suisan fish market and along the Wailoa river bridge to wait for the tsunami. Some worried that there would be nothing to see. At 1.04 a.m., when the Settlement Clock stopped forever, they were overwhelmed by a nearly vertical wall of water more that twenty feet high.

At the Pirates' 75th anniversary banquet last year, one of the guests of honour was nonagenarian Mrs Ito, the most renowned survivor of the destruction of Waiakea. Her home had been uprooted by the wave, then sucked out to sea by its rip tide. Unable to swim and less that five feet tall, she clung all night to a flimsy window screen, surrounded by hammerhead sharks, before being rescued in the morning by the Coast Guard. Weaker characters might boast of the ordeal, but Mrs Ito, with superb humility, simply recalled the indelible beauty of the star-jewelled night sky as she floated in the ocean.

Old Waiakea, thanks to the Pirates, also seems indelible. The oral histories and public recollections of the 1960 tragedy, together with the publication last spring of a town and team memoir by Richard Nakamura and Gloria Kobayashi, have rekindled its descendants' abiding affection. Waiakea's militant labour history, on the other hand, has been largely excluded from commemoration. There is no memorial to the victims of the 1938 massacre, and, although the local ILWU hall is named after Harry Kamoku, there is an unsurprising tendency—in the absence of any strong union participation in the making of public memory—to stress 'unifying' experiences like natural disasters or sports legends rather than 'divisive' legacies of racism or class struggle.

3. Laupahoehoe School

At Laupahoehoe, however, five generations of labour in the cane fields and sugar mills remain the pivot of community identity. Frank DeCaires, who was fourteen years old in 1946 when two sisters and a brother were swept away by a tsunami exactly where he is now sitting, at the grassy tip of breathtaking Laupahoehoe Point, is talking about mules. 'We used mules in those days, you know, to help us bring the cane down slope. They were good animals and they worked hard, just like the rest of us. Sugar was a difficult way of life,

but it made us into a family, close-knit and generous.'

The kids sitting at his feet, a typical Hawaiian rainbow of half a dozen intermixed ethnicities, smile or nod. Mules are not a comprehensible category, but the tall sugar stalks growing wild in abandoned fields everywhere along the Hamakua Coast are like a distant relation. They are ancestral pride. None of these children will ever pull a graveyard shift in the Pepeekeo Mill or haul tons of cane through a tropical cloudburst in an eighteen-wheeled Peterbilt. But their parents and grandparents did, just as their parents and grandparents before them cut the treacherous cane by hand and hauled it on their backs to wagons or flumes. Cane is family history and a subject deserving respect.

April 1, 1999: a chance to see first-hand how history is transmitted on the Big Island. The Laupahoehoe School (or, rather, the 'new school', several hundred feet above the ocean) has organised a day-long commemoration of the 1946 tragedy. Although it is a weekday, a majority of Laupahoehoe's 152 families have come out to the Point. Since the final sugar harvest here in the fall of 1994, unemployment has skyrocketed and the school has become more than ever the centre of community life. As adults prepare lunch or trade gossip, students of all grades gather in 'talk-story' tents to listen to honoured kūpuna (elders) like DeCaires recollect about work and disaster.

In 1996 and 1997, students transcribed and published a remarkable narrative based on interviews with thirteen tsunami survivors. It is chilling to hear the kūpuna tell yet again how the sea suddenly retreated, leaving the ocean shelf exposed as far as the reef. It was 6.50 a.m., ten minutes before the first bell, and school buses were discharging kids from nearby plantation camps and hamlets. Some were playing baseball. Unconscious of the danger, they ran to the shore just beyond the teachers' cottages to view the shoals of fish writhing on the sea bed. Before adults could recall them to safety, the main swell arrived: not a breaking wave, but an ever-rising, ever-encroaching wall of water.

Leonie Kawaihona Laeha, interviewed by students in 1996, remembers that '"it was very high, coming, like, over the coconut trees. All the kids who had been down by the beach were running up the road and through the park." When she saw that, she started to cry because she "didn't realize what was happening, but just knew it was bad."' Nearby, sixteen-year-old Yasu Gusukuma, 'gripped by a horror that would remain forever in her memory', witnessed 'water coming from all sides of the point and "boiling" in the centre. She saw cottages spinning on top of the water, she saw the grandstand collapse, then she turned and ran up the hill as fast as she could.'

Some of the children, like DeCaires' adopted sister, Janet Yokoyama, were killed instantly as the tsunami dashed them against rocks and trees. More than a dozen others were swept alive into the shark-infested waters. 'Some of the boys tried to swim out, tied to ropes, and grab people floating by, but weren't able to reach any. They helplessly watched many float by.'

As the screaming kids were sucked out to sea, David Kailimai, superintendent at a neighbouring sugar mill, tried to borrow the area's only sailboat from a wealthy *haole*

resident. More concerned about possible damage to his boat than the lost children, the owner stubbornly refused. It was 1.00 p.m., six hours after the disaster, before he finally relented. Kailimai, a doctor from the plantation clinic, and two others sailed north toward Kohala through an incredible junkyard of floating debris. Before nightfall they were able to rescue two injured boys clinging to a luahala tree and a school teacher who had reached one of the rubber rafts dropped by Navy planes. The teacher was the doctor's fiancée. Three more children were rescued the next morning, but others, 'seen on makeshift rafts down the coast', were never found.

After an hour or two of such stories, everyone converges on the impressive community centre (built for a much larger population in the heyday of the Laupahoehoe Sugar Company) for a feast of luau pig, rice and poi. A few older people poke around sadly in the vine-covered ruins of the elementary kids' restrooms destroyed in 1946: the tiny, rusted sinks are especially poignant. Then the assembled community, led by the school honour guard, marches down to the modest lava monument engraved with the names of the dead children and their young teachers. There is a moving hymn in Hawaiian, ecumenical prayers from Catholics, Mormons and Buddhists, and then the principal, Jane Uyehara, reminds her students that the Point itself, 'this beautiful, special place', is God's grace on the dead. Surrounded on three sides by thundering surf, it is indeed a magnificent monument.

It is also a long way from Littleton, Colorado, and other suburban infernos. When asked what careers they imagine for themselves, half the kids reply they want to be teachers at the School. Teachers, like those who died trying to save children from the monstrous wave in 1946, are still heroes. (Hawaiians, it should be noted, have always cherished education. In the 1880s, when it was still an independent nation, Hawai'i had an astonishing 96 per cent literacy rate: higher than the United States in the year 2000.) But many of these kids, inexorably, will be forced to leave Laupahoehoe.

Despite tax-funded schemes to turn displaced sugar workers into taro farmers or to re-employ them as low-wage 'teleworkers' processing credit-card billings from the mainland, there are no longer enough jobs to sustain the entire community. Residents are bitterly divided over the jobs-versus-traditional-values proposal to build a maximum-security prison outside Hilo (the governor's alternative is to export Hawai'i's felons to private prisons in Texas). Over time, more ageing malihini (like myself) from California will discover the romance of the Hamakua Coast and supplant many of the local families who will, in turn, end up in the sprawling, troubled outskirts of Los Angeles or Las Vegas. This is the true 'cloud of sadness', as one local writer put it, that hangs over the Big Island.

Husk

They live
in a little house.

They eat oysters

and other molluscs
reputed to enhance
love.

    ★

Outside
gleaming shells
of cicadas

their amber crackling

grass fire
underfoot.

    ★

His soft voice
nursing lust

raw with emotion.

Passion
and twilight

in the dark
shadows
beneath his eyes.

She lights
the paper lantern

a cape gooseberry
dangles
from her fingers

    ★

or perhaps the shell
of a man

delicate skin

a silk purse
for the mulberry
stem

the hungry life
within.

    ★

But she is tired.

Little
hollow
pod—

nut with
the sweet
meat
gone.

*

A father's kiss
goodnight—

hairy wooden cheek

coconut
lightly sanding

smelling of the sea.

*

Drawn up
on a shelly beach

the hull of a small
craft, a coracle

sun sinking gloomily
in the bay

the monks returning
to their island hermitage.

*

But look—
an arrival!

A fruit boat
has been bobbing
for days across the ocean

its green message
come to rest on this dumb
hospitable shore.

     *

They have known each other
for some time.

Months
have passed
in the little house
where she stands
at the window

hearing the cough
of a young bullock
turned out to forage
in stubble

its tongue
protruding suddenly

in the winter dusk.
Dry honk
of a saxophone.
The smoky air.

She runs her hands
through silky
corngold hair

    ★

as a dog barks way
beyond the timberline

a rough-coated dog,
in language
of the northern tundra.

In saltier times
the skin of the dog-fish
was used
for smoothing arrows

    ★

and now
the shark beneath the skin
wants out.

It wants to shuck her
and swim free

heedless
in its sharp teeth

and sandpaper
capsule.

She bites down.
She holds his hand.
She opens up

    ★

and up
and here

the new one comes—
sharp no more

their little shellfish
now without a shell.

She lies back—
scooped out

cocooned.
My love

he says

my sweet
husk.

PETER WELLS

The Earache

Often I had earaches as a child. They would come on suddenly, like a fre-
quency I had tuned into. Because I was familiar with the terror they brought, I
would often ignore these opening tweaks of tenderness inside my eardrum. I
pretended nothing was happening. As time went on and the situation within
my family grew more complex, I became very adept at this sort of pretence.
After a while it came naturally to me. So it was nothing for me to keep riding
my bike home, to open the back door of the house with the key, then enter the
silence, which always had about it an animus, a watching waiting feeling.
Once home, though, I could collapse. Whatever tender or fragile collection of
improbabilities I had constructed for a self, encased as it was in the tough
fibre of my skin, could evaporate instantly. I became defined, instead, by the
bread bin, by the fridge in which I would find the butter in summer, and my
greatest pleasure of all, a tin of golden syrup.

If I had to offer an image of the pleasures of boyhood, it would be a door-
step of fresh white bread, wedges of chilled butter pressed down hard into it.
I was impatient to begin gorging. I had a growing boy's insensate, even
sensational, spasms of hunger—hunger like an hallucination, or the with-
drawal of a drug. I felt that I had only just made it to the bread bin in time.
One of the most beautiful things I ever saw was a swimming tide of golden
syrup. Was it that I was evading reality, or trying to replace one reality with
another, that I saw one thing only as I gazed down at the golden syrup, bread
and butter?

This was the literally gorgeous cloak of gold which the Queen wore at
some point in her coronation. As I gazed down, in that terrible, tender
moment before I fed it into my mouth—my jaws clicking open, with an
audible crack of desire—I always had a vivid, almost hallucinatory flare in
which I briefly felt I was eating cloth of gold, ermine. Perhaps this is another

way of saying that aesthetics provided a dubious, but at the time comforting, anaesthetic against pain.

But the fact was, even as I fed the bread and golden syrup into me, I was aware, almost subcutaneously, of a residual wire of pain, burning . . . This might be a special kind of tenderness in the bowl of the inner ear. It might feel as if some sort of gruel was roiling to the boil. I did my best to ignore these signs. I would continue on my trancing way, into my room, to get changed. Maybe to get my tennis racket out and go outside to the garage doors where I might spend several hours rallying, improving my service, in my imagination sending back wonderful backhanders, mentally acknowledging the cheers of the crowd, or absorbing the admiring look of a boy I particularly wanted to impress.

Hours would evaporate. Standing on the same spot, I seemed to feel time rushing past me, my future life, almost, pressing up so close I could feel it, a wetness brushing my face.

Pain quickly comes to animate itself. It ceases to be abstract. Eventually mine became so severe that there was no ignoring it. This escalation brought with it a terror that was absolute. I knew now I was in for a long period of stasis. Time had lifted off me, like a set of clothes I no longer needed. I would be naked with this pain. Located inside the skull, it was an incandescent worm, eating everything within me which was human until I was left as a kind of X-ray of an elemental being, like a boy found, say, in an ossuary or archaeological dig. Thus would begin my travail.

It was caused, of course, by swimming. As the beach nearby became more polluted, so the abscesses inside my ears grew worse. One year there was an especially bad earache. I ended up at the hospital—the main hospital in town, by the Domain. I was convinced I would be left behind there, cast off as the unwanted child I always suspected I was. My mother was with me. I usually had an injection in my leg, I suppose a painkiller. (I have no memory of the abscesses being lanced. None.)

This year the nurse could not find a vein in my leg despite repeated insertions of the needle. Perhaps my fright communicated itself to my mother. The most powerful effect of my earaches was that they rearranged spatial dimensions. The world receded into the excruciating nerve-ending that was screaming inside my head. Everyone was far away. The person I loved most in the world, my mother, could do nothing to help me. In fact I could say that I first became identified as myself through these experiences of earache. Everyone I knew, even the person who meant most to me, seemed to slip away down a darkened corridor, become miniatures of themselves, helpless, hopeless.

For the first time in my life, my own thingness was unavoidable.

I have a succinct memory of that hospital room. I know the block within the hospital where this incident occurred. There was a small high window of glazed white glass. The concrete walls were painted dun-green. A nurse is bent over me. I am being stoic. Stoicism, rather than heroism, is at times the only refuge left. I had resigned my body anyway. It had, after all, betrayed me. I felt I was being lowered into a huge machine in which I only had vestigial rights. The needle, which appeared so glittering and long, became the image of my pain. Localised, it took on, adopted, the physicality of the earache, gave the pain a shape.

The needle sank in. The nurse was sweating at her failure. I could smell her acrid body, like metal fatigue. Everything was washing off, all her belief in her ability to effect change, mute pain. The needle withdrew. She hurriedly swabbed my thigh—blood smudged onto cotton wool. Ethyl. She began again.

What is so strange about all this is that I sensed one thing above all others: my mother's mute distress. I could see her sitting beside me, being brave for me but watching as the needle slid in again. I could sense the bracing of her body, almost hear the heart in her body beating savagely with a mother's pain that she could not absorb my pain, deliver me from my hurt. In some sense I felt I was betraying her by not allowing her to absorb my pain. A curious illogic, but one which I adopted because I could sense, without understanding, that she was experiencing a great pain of motherhood: to have given birth, to have created something out of herself, yet in the end be unable to protect that being from the misfortunes of life, of which this earache could only be said to be an introductory echo.

Finally, on that long-ago afternoon, a vein was found. Slowly the painkiller rose in a muffling tide, cooling the worm which had made itself at home inside my skull. Soon it would be all over. I would be returned to my body, its betrayals reversed. Again I would be the growing boy who every so often had an earache.

Curiously, it was on this occasion that the doctor, perhaps unnerved by so much hysteria, lanced the abscess a little carelessly and perforated my eardrum. I became partially deaf in my left ear at the age of twelve. It never occurred to my parents to protest about this and I grew up with this defect. It made swimming difficult, because the logic ran that the hole in my ear would allow germs to breed, hence another abscess. My mother tried to make me wear a bathing cap, to keep the water out. I did try this once, but it was more than my sexual confusion could cope with. So I stopped swimming.

Many years later, I took up swimming again. I was always careful not to let water get into my ear. Even as a man of thirty, then forty, I did not want to get an earache. The archetype of extreme pain—the most extreme pain I've known in my life—stands as that earache.

As time went on, I became concerned that my hearing was deteriorating. I went for a test. I explained my childhood experience to the doctor—elliptically, in a few wry sentences. He peered within for a time.

Then he turned the little light off and said to me, almost in passing, that there was no evidence my eardrum had ever been perforated.

Mysteries

It had been a packed and late commuter train, but now they were past Waterloo, and the carriage was suddenly empty. Only Christina and the foreign-looking gentleman remained. Although she was not to know, his heavy grey overcoat concealed both his bulk and his wings. Huge black wings, swan wings bound up with tape, taped to his body. Old wings, arthritic wings, made uncomfortable for the sake of appearances.

Got-cha got-cha got-cha, said the train.

GOT-CHA GOT-CHA GOT-CHA, added the tunnel.

Night and the lights turned the windows into mirrors, reflecting nothing in particular, empty seats, and the angel, and herself. He approached her, the way she hoped that strangers wouldn't on public transportation. He had terrible shadows beneath his eyes, six thousand workaday shades of purple, one for every year he had been watching over the world. He bore a coarse and careless stubble too, darkening his cheeks and hiding deep pockmarks.

Hello, he said.

He tipped his hat to her. How foreign, how peculiar, she thought, staring, not wanting to stare because she knew it was rude, but he wanted her attention, she was sure. He cleared his throat in confirmation.

Uh, hello, she said, not meaning it.

Mary, he said, and he meant it as a title, for it was only her middle name. His hand was on her shoulder, pressing heavily against her like a holy relic. I am the angel Gabriel, he said. You are pregnant. He said it like a doctor, although she suspected even insects could understand him. A moth caught in the carriage turned from the fascination of a light, stared at her. You are pregnant with three children, he said. You will keep their divinity from harm.

Gabriel, is that a Jewish name? she thought, and he alighted, it was his station.

She walked home in the dewy cold, in the falling darkness, pondering. The unmiraculous angel's touch weighed on her shoulder and moved through her, ink in water, getting heavier, knotting her insides. She imagined her belly swelling, imagined dressing in preggy clothes, sweatshirts and tracksuits and oversize skirts. Like the mothers in the mall, pushing two grubs in a buggy and expecting another. They looked happy and sad at the same time.

She had never been good at school, and was unsurprised when she failed her pregnancy test three times in a row. She called her boss and said that she had been diagnosed, that she would have to leave. Aw, you're a bloody silly girl, he said. She imagined his moustache moving irritably as she put down the phone.

She liked pregnancy at first, the way her hands were no longer raw and red from industrial-strength lavatory cleaners. Her skin cleared up, but never glowed in the manner she hoped it might. She went to free antenatal aquarobic classes and got books from the library illustrated with scientific cutaways and gory births.

She called her mother to break the news, unsuccessfully. She was reminded of her dear dead father's prophecy that she would never come to anything. Pregnancy was often the consequence of underperformance in school, of leaving early, of not chewing correctly, and especially of wearing too much make-up. Chrissie closed her eyes very hard when her mother, an emphatic woman, emphatically hung up. She did not open them for a whole minute.

After six months, she still believed it was an immaculate conception, although her friends told her stories about foreign women who sat on public toilet seats the wrong way. Disturbing images of alien sperm sticking to her thighs in a cubicle, reaching for her insides, played against the back of her skull. Stranger things have happened, they said, and she agreed, but was uncomforted by the sure knowledge that truth was stranger than fiction. She couldn't manage out at the pub with them. The toilets there were horrible, and she ended up staring at the wall-mounted television in silence.

She stayed at home for the next two months, sometimes calling in to talkback radio, not that she saw herself as the opinionated sort. It was company, for she kept to herself. Her three babies moved like fish in her womb, pressing against her belly-skin, which seemed thinner every day, until it was as tenuous as the surface of an ocean. Little hands only just held inside her reached for air and little feet kicked, submarine earthquakes.

On Christmas Eve, an hour before midnight, she knew that her children would arrive a full month early, that it was almost time. She sat lonely at a bar, staring at the televised city of Christchurch singing carols in a park. The candle lights were pretty.

Little donkey, little donkey words trailed across the bottom of the screen. She downed her fourth double bourbon and turned to the man next to her. Hello, she said.

Merry Christmas, he said, like a greetings card. He was pear-like, with stubby, merry features, and premature baldness undelayed by a number of pharmacy-only remedies.

Yes, she said.

I'm Raymond.

Hi.

Who're you?

Chrissie.

Another? he said, with the kind of misjudged suavity that comes from practising in front of a mirror before leaving the house.

Um, yes. Yes please.

Raymond gestured to his good friend Harry behind the bar, and returned his smile to her. Have you got any Lithuanian in you? he asked. It was always worth a shot.

She laughed. He laughed. All she could say was Please help me, please help me, as her waters broke.

She would not go to the hospital. It was filled with forms printed in medical colours, and Merry Christmas accidents. She could not speak the secret language of forms, but they had words and a grammar that could define her with sharp, surgical precision.

A tiny star shone over Raymond's tiny bedsit. Contractions hit her, cruel as fists, for two hours. Raymond held her hands tightly in his own. She gave birth to a boy and a girl, both holy. The two were too perfect to be her own, only partly human, but she loved them. Their eyes reflected angels or the fairy lights on Raymond's tree. And then she gave birth to a third child that she knew was wholly hers, for it was unradiant and squinted just like she did. It was neither a boy nor a girl. Where the sexual organs should have been, there was nothing, only a smooth mound, like a doll's.

What's that, asked Raymond, exhausted from boiling water, and fetching towels, and all the other things they did on television when they were caught delivering babies unexpectedly. He cut the umbilici with a pair of kitchen scissors, his own improvisation. What's that?

He's a boy, she insisted, for she had always wanted a little boy to call her own. She loved him, although she did not know where he came from. It was a mystery unmentioned in the body of thought on virgin births.

Raymond slept on the floor, a perfect gentleman in a stale sleeping bag and summer pyjamas. She lay on his divan, fidgeted with distant anxieties about swimming pools and toilet seats, feeling too old and tired. She held two golden children from heaven and one ordinary boy asleep in her arms, and stared at strange wallpaper. And at the unfamiliar tinsel tree, with Raymond's present to himself sitting underneath it, a wrapped bottle. He had written on the small to-and-from card, in a graceless hand, King Raymond was not a good man . . .

She watched them, waiting for human colour to move through their bodies, tiny and fragile as miracles. Nobody came with gifts for them, or played for them, or knelt before them. Instead, she quietly pa-rumpa-pum-pummed for them, barely humming because she didn't want to wake Raymond, the red-nosed midwife who had been so kind. He accompanied her with resonant snores. The children's arrival was barely acknowledged; they were meant to be a secret.

It is difficult to keep secrets in a modern democracy.

Taxi drivers infer or divulge. Smiling prime-time presenters tittle-tattle. What began as supposition or conjecture becomes hearsay, hearsay becomes a little-known fact, which in turn becomes Common Knowledge, which is explained in the editorial pages of the daily papers.

Christina watched the radio, listened to magazines, read the television.

I have a recurrent dream where two babies with skin like copper are sleeping at the centre of the earth. They wake and stretch their arms out to the periphery of the world, and grasp it, and pull it to pieces as they emerge from the amniotic magma, wrote Anxious Pisces, Blenheim. So did Mel's Gran of Hawera. So did Perturbed Leo of Auckland.

This is a very complicated question, this messianic birth, the radio reported. It paused to remind Christina that at this stage, there was no reason to think of it as anything other than a possibility. She held her children closer to her. There were issues of hygiene, parental responsibility, proper notification and certification, and the social erosion represented by solo motherhood.

Some meat-packers insisted that they had seen a heavenly host with angry eyes and flaming brands on Christmas Eve. They had been too drunk to do anything at the time, but were happy to have an infotaining and entermational televisual documentary made about their experience.

Newsreaders dropped their smiles to show they were serious and presented compelling new evidence that there had been a divine parturition. The Political Editor examined the Prime Minister's response. No government can tolerate the possibility of unauthorised messianic activity, or the social erosion that is associated with a birth of this nature, she said.

Where is this child or children? cried the Public. This is not hygienic, this is not right, we need transparency, accountability; this is not Christian, added the letters page of every newspaper.

There were green papers, then white ones, a committee process abandoned to urgency. A democratic massacre of the innocents seemed unfortunate, but inevitable. An oh-eight-hundred number was set up, along with an explanatory campaign of television advertisements. A special working group was established, doctors and constables, social workers and butchers. Death certificates were to be mailed out within eight working days.

Christina Mary had never been good at school, but she was not a fool, and she was mindful of her promise. She went to a secret river she knew, wrapped her twins up warm, and cast them adrift in an unusually seaworthy cot she had purchased from the Salvation Army. They looked back at her with perfect baby faces, fresh and new. And they might have whispered, although later she could not be sure, that inside every tree there is a green river, unconscious, slow and oozing. They might have whispered this together and in perfect unison. The river begins in the earth and reaches out to the sun. In every man and woman there is the instinct to stand tall, reach towards a Kingdom.

And they were gone, washed away, bobbed away, and baptised by rivers and oceans slapping against the sides of the cot, over it. Water rested like cold jewels on their holy faces. She imagined them drifting out to where the sky wept quietly into the ocean. They had given her their first parable and she kept it secret with her river.

The Parliamentary Taskforce came to her door, February the 28th. There were seven of them. There was a social worker to explain things, two community constables—there had been some trouble with the scheme—two young doctors to pronounce the children dead, a nurse, just in case, and an experienced slaughterman. They were all dressed in smart casual clothes styled not to upset or unsettle. Only the slaughterman and the nurse wore butcher's aprons. They looked like television chefs and waited demurely behind the other five. She was waiting, with her final child, standing like a wooden icon in her front doorway. The roses and the camellia in her little yard heard her speak with them. The social worker asked politely for her three children.

No, I have only one baby, she said.

It says here that you have three, Christina, said the social worker, measured, stabbing papers on her clipboard with her index finger.

I have only one.

Your case notes say three. She indicated a computer-generated form, deadly accurate.

But I only have one, said Christina, trying not to cry.

I'll have to check.

You can go through the house. Honestly.

We'd need a separate warrant for that. The policemen looked uncomfortable behind her.

Just take him. He's all I've got, just take him.

I realise that this is difficult for you, Christina, we're all trying—

Just kill him, please, just go away. She shouted at them, called them bastards and bitches. Her neighbours started peeking like ghosts from behind netted curtains and trimmed hedges.

The Taskforce was running late anyway, so they took her final boy. The social worker asked her to look away. She didn't. A doctor and the nurse held him to the ground, in case his two months struggled, and the slaughterman released a sprung bolt into his brain. He was examined and pronounced dead. They left him in the driveway, staining the concrete as if his blood were ink, then climbed into their van and headed up the street to 42A.

Her neighbours brought her tiny child inside, wrapped in a towel to keep out the cold, made her tea, and didn't know what to say. I will not vote for this government again, they thought, but kept it to themselves.

If she needed anything, they said. She said she was all right, thank you, she couldn't say how grateful she was. So they left. She needed some time to herself, they said. It was probably the best thing.

Her tea went cold and the light had gone out of the day. Slowly, and in her own time, she remembered each of her secrets and her only mystery.

PAOLA BILBROUGH

Erosion

Throat locked against joy she wore
hot afternoons like heavy, unwelcome garments.

Severing roses from strangers' bushes,
passing through endless corridors of streets.

It seemed the men on corners were rolling
cigarettes with sheaves of human skin.

The sky murky; a badly executed watercolour
she was not at liberty to fold away.

We were rarely alone; there was the blond
boy in the fedora and old men's suits.

His instruments lined the hall: cello
leaning against guitar, French horn by itself.

What he was to her I could not tell.
She in white linen, light as a gourd, he in black wool.

In the near dark of the rented house her bones
shone faintly blue, ribs a fish skeleton, flesh picked out.

Nights when the rest of the city lay bare,
she was ironed flat beneath two feather quilts,

sunken cheeks, hair oiled, twisted off her face.
I could not halt her body's willing erosion

nor pull myself from the mould of sulky, anxious child.
Late at night I would step from my lover's bed,

cross the motorway, arrive at my mother's house.
She lying under the wings of a wooden bird with iron feet.

There were flowers dropping petals, furred quinces.
Lemons surrounded by leaves over the mantelpiece.

Face pressed against the back of her neck,
awaiting sleep I knew that she would go.

The walls were full of widening cracks
and I heard the soft movement of earth falling.

Watchtowers

Laurence Aberhart

Toi Shan, China: 1929 and 1954

The slightly inland region of Toi Shan in Western Guangdong province in China was a source of massive emigration in the late 19th and early 20th centuries, supplying a majority of the Chinese emigrants who eventually settled in the USA, Australia, Canada and New Zealand.

Toi Shan sits just outside the recent industrial belt of factories, new towns and concrete that runs like a vast wedge between Hong Kong, Macau and Guangzhou. This region has undergone probably the greatest topographic transformation of any region in the world since 1991. Villages once sustained by agriculture have been razed or absorbed to accommodate vast factory complexes, worker dormitories, shoddy, quickly constructed, concrete-slabbed shops, and high-rise buildings more befitting a Manhatten skyline. The hazy sky is endless and fences dense with text promote the benefits of both mobile phones and the one child policy.

In an earlier economic boom—the '20s one—Toi Shan benefited from the successes of its distant former residents. Money and families repatriated, and a building boom brought distinctive European-inspired shop-houses to the cities. In the surrounding countryside, however, smaller villages maintained traditional styles and building materials. Homes with distinctive curved roofs (reputedly to allow dragons a comfortable rest) were extended, rebuilt and modernised. The ultimate status symbol was an attached watchtower with storage areas for valuables. The recently returned expatriates, however, had memories of their homeland that were thirty years out of date. The pirates, bandits and robbers of an earlier era had disappeared and the watchtowers were never used for their intended purpose . . . Similar, I suppose, to the nuclear air-raid shelters that proliferated in China during the Cold War of the '50s.

—John Batten

Titles of images (in order of appearance):

Watchtower, near Toi Shan, Guangdong Province, China, 27 November 2000.

Village and Watchtower, Guangdong Province, China, 27 November 2000.

Watchtower and Pavilion, Guangdong Province, China, 27 November 2000.

Watchtower, Wong Di Village, Guangdong Province, China, 27 November 2000.

JANET CHARMAN

backnote

i take The Unit
into the bulgy hills

walk from the station
through the carry me streets

our
place

has gone back something terrific

a broken car on the grass
just grass
the peeling paint
even the new part

where we went
to see next door's
television
and Dad said
we're not getting one

or the night he leant
over the fire
face buried
in folded arms

and I on the turned down mat
looked up
sure
it's ringing in him
the toll call

my father's gone

asking her
sitting in the chair
was it that?

no
she replied

Dad's cold

plum pud

only enough for one   your turn will come

plum   pud

sitting in
a straight back chair
part of the gloom of tar paper and nogs
that form the wall innards

    plum   pud

here and there day
light violates the corrugated iron
getting in for nothing

      plum   pud

with a wallow
in a box of dust
their slippers
readied for the floor
of the strange garage

        plum   pud

their feet
refer to the shape of a step
their arms
rising in the dimness
gracing
the five positions

         plum   pud

the absent car
does it defer to the bodies' mysteries?

          plum   pud

the teacher's heights
driving them to the circle
skirts
the moves across
the arabesques and then she won't let me stay and watch

           plumpud
            who won? let's do it again

pud   plum

FELICITY MILBURN

Building Sites:
Hotere's Sculpitecture

Man is
a great wall builder . . .
but the wall most impregnable
has a moat
flowing with fright
around his heart.
—Oswald Mtshali (from 'Walls', in *Sounds of a Cowhide Drum*, 1971)

Investigators of the work of Ralph Hotere are often mesmerised by its poetic lyricism and dark, alchemic beauty. Yet there is another, neglected, quality at the heart of Hotere's best work, a raw, rustic physicality that is as concerned with the ground on which we walk and shelter as with any flights of soul or thought. This bedrock interest in materiality and structure, manifested most obviously in his characteristic use of salvaged and industrial materials, is surprisingly constant in the work of an artist so celebrated for his manipulations of shadow, allusion and apparent emptiness. Certainly, it's an interest on which the contributors to the catalogue of the survey exhibition *Black Light* (initiated by the Dunedin Public Art Gallery and The Museum of New Zealand Te Papa Tongarewa and exhibited in Auckland, Wellington and Dunedin in 2000–2001) are oddly silent; I want to pursue the building metaphor in Hotere's major works and to see what kind of pressure it will bear.

Colonial sash-window frames, demolition timber, lead-head nails, corrugated iron and stainless steel—Hotere's use of such materials invites comparison with the Italian *arte povera* movement in its deliberate and minimalist use of humble, 'non-art' materials. Yet the use he makes of those materials reveals a desire to locate the work not only in the thick of the everyday (non-art) world, but also amidst New Zealand's vernacular architecture, and in particular in the landscapes of coastal Otago. In sculptures such as *Pathway to the Sea—Aramoana* (1991) and *P.R.O.P.* (1991), Hotere (with collaborator Bill Culbert) uses vernacular forms and objects to earth his works in the politics and aesthetics of his local environment. Crucially, the power of these works lies not in their evocation of a misty elsewhere—an elsewhere which Hotere's advocates often squint to see—but from their creation of a real space, inhabited bodily, in the here and now. These structures, one sees, not only evoke places, they *are* places. Built, painted, sliced, burred and polished into existence around both artist and spectator, they are foundations on which to stand and from which to resist.

By now the calendar of Hotere's career is well-known—the development of a reductivist style in the '60s during and after studies at the Central School of Art in London, the extension of that style in later decades in expressive and politicised directions. But it was in the '80s that Hotere began to salvage local forms and materials in earnest. Made in 1981, *Black Window (Towards Aramoana)* is an early example. A luminescent white cross shines out of a soft black ground, the contrast between them tempered by a section of variegated tonal markings across the base and the jumbled letters and numerals that occupy the top-left corner. By placing this composition in an old, unpainted sash-window frame, Hotere lends it a sensual richness, but also an abrupt physicality—the frame's presence offering up the possibility that one could pass from looking into participating, that this is a world to be opened and entered, rather than merely beheld. Hotere brings the frame into the everyday, expanding its relevance to life in the here and now, invoking, then dismantling, the idea of the picture frame as a signifier of 'art space', as identified by Roger Shattuck in 1961:

> The frame, the conventional rectangular window of a painting, lays out a universe within which the multiple relationships are self-sufficient and fill the space to the edges . . . Confronting such a work, even if it portrays a bloody massacre, or a sinner, or the ecstasy of a saint, one is not personally importuned to react. Its architectural balance and the dramatic isolation establish the proper distance.

In modifying this traditional division to encompass an agenda of participation—the act of looking *through* rather than the passivity of looking *at*—Hotere demands not only attention but involvement, placing the call for solidarity at our door. This is as true of his overtly political works such as the *Polaris* series as it is of more private and inward-turning paintings like *Night Window, Carey's Bay* (1995). The full force of these works is felt when they are gathered in groups of three or more, whereupon they seem to summon up the architectural ghost of the house they might once have inhabited. The neutral space of the air-conditioned white cube starts to echo with other histories. Together, the *Black Windows* might be seen as a portable chapel, components of a moving house. The humanising effect of the recycled timber framing is perhaps best revealed in *Night Window*'s opposite number, the glossy, water-smooth black-painted surround of the Culbert and Hotere collaboration *Post Black #13* (1992). Here the frame, stripped of the individualising marks of time and use, has become a modernist statement, a gleaming enclosure for the shaft of artificial light at its centre. It does not so much guide you in as reflect upon you—a fundamentally self-contained manifesto.

Hotere's use of the wooden frame and his employment of (and allusions to) other vernacular building materials and practices are, for me, symptoms of a desire to create structure. By 'structure' I mean something less abstract than formal order, although Hotere's early works are some of the most eloquent expressions of formal order in New Zealand art. Hotere's works are, rather, offered as shelters, supports, barricades and footholds.

Ralph Hotere and Bill Culbert, *P.R.O.P.*, 1991, mixed media, collection Dunedin Public Art Gallery. Photograph: Bill Nichol.

The works are examples of what's been called 'sculpitecture'—objects raised in a charged mid-ground between building and art, a space where the distinction between what a building is and what a building protects starts to blur in troublesome and beautiful ways. This impulse reaches its climax in the large installations P.R.O.P., Black Phoenix and Pathway to the Sea—Aramoana, but it is also present in less obviously constructed works, where matter meets matter and both hover on what Francis Pound calls 'a perpetual threshold of disappearance'.

It is in the Black Paintings sequence of 1968 that Hotere's interest in structure is most simply, if covertly, expressed. Seven black mirrors; seven radiant crosses; seven singular paintings—a grouping as resolved and complete as the days of a week. The seven phases of the prismatic spectrum—red, orange, yellow, green, blue, indigo and violet—bind the black like gateways, holding the silence taut at our approach. If these works possess a spiritual quality, as many commentators have suggested, it is in their dedication to the act of creation, in the most pragmatic sense. For within the lines of a linear Greek cross, a shape that denotes the most fundamental act of building by placing a vertical form into and through a horizontal base, the artist has quietly assembled the building blocks of light. And as Petrus Van der Velden, romantic patriarch of the New Zealand landscape sublime, would have it: Colour is Light—Light is Love—Love is God.

In an interview in the Black Light exhibition catalogue, artist John Reynolds refers to Hotere's reinvention of domestic and industrial forms, and specifically to his 'summoning [of] the conventions of materials through transgressions'. The artist's unorthodox approach to materials—butting a sash-window frame onto a viewless gallery wall, arranging the wrecked limbs of a fishing boat into a motionless shrine—seems only to reinforce our consciousness of their origins. This strategy was most obviously revealed in No 8: an installation (1992), in which the artist filled the gallery of RKS Art with the glinting tangle of nearly eight kilometres of fencing wire. Even as he explored the bounding, boundless beauty of a material that had, in his words, been 'wrapped around this country for many years', Hotere's playfulness only underscored the wire's usual function: to secure, retain and control. As light and loose as it appeared, the wire continued to dictate entry into, and movement within, the space, fencing it off as surely as if strainer posts had occupied each corner.

Corrugated iron was first intended, and is most commonly used, as a roofing material, but in Hotere's hands it takes on other functions, whilst maintaining a quality of impenetrable solidity. In Blackwater (1999) it becomes a vast meniscus of peaty water; in the Aramoana panels (1982), a resolute palisade fence-line; and in P.R.O.P. (1991), a defiant retaining wall. In many works, the material's temporary, makeshift quality contributes to the pervading atmosphere of urgency, voicing the threat of danger and imminent collapse. This is particularly evident in P.R.O.P., a collaboration with Culbert that takes its title from the name of the Society for the Protection of Observation Point, a group established to prevent the obliteration of Observation Point by the Otago Harbour Board in 1989 to clear space for a railway and timber operation.

Ralph Hotere, *Aramoana*, 1982 (detail), lacquer on corrugated iron, wood, collection Auckland Art Gallery Toi o Tāmaki.
Photograph: Jennifer French.

Bitter resistance to the plan was finally unsuccessful, and the Board had its way in 1989, wiping out a number of private buildings, including Hotere's studio. The positioning of alternating blue and white fluorescent tubes at equidistant intervals in the undulating iron, as well as the sleek industrial lacquer finish and sheer physicality of the work, bring to mind the monumental mass of Donald Judd's modular rolled steel slab works of the late '60s. Like Judd, Hotere wants to convey the physical reality of the materials. But, in bracing contrast to Judd's insistence that his sculptures resisted any social or political agenda—that they were nothing more than the sum of their physical parts—P.R.O.P. is an emphatic, and eloquent, metaphor for the act of holding your ground.

Sharing more than merely a similarity of title with Richard Serra's propped lead works of the '60s, most notably *One Ton Prop (House of Cards)* and *Corner Prop* (both 1969), Hotere and Culbert's *P.R.O.P.* concentrates the viewer's attention on the sheer mass of its construction, the precarious black slope suggesting the heady weight of a hillside propped up and held back by a retaining wall of corrugated iron. Yet even as it places the viewer at the point of least security in the event of a collapse, the work becomes a structure of resistance, a point of momentary stability in which to regroup. Whereas Serra's malevolently insecure works exist entirely as an evocation of the inevitability of collapse, P.R.O.P. becomes a celebration of the nobility of a last stand against an irresistible force bent on destruction. In this context, Hotere seems to suggest, building becomes an act of faith.

But before resistance comes resilience, of which no sculpture is a better embodiment than the much celebrated and immutably moving *Black Phoenix* (1984–88). Constructed from the salvaged remains of *The Poitrel*, a burnt-out fishing boat, the installation is an awesome monument to faith and survival. Held upright shoulder to shoulder along the gallery wall, thirty blistered and scorched timber sections flank the central prow like a guard of honour, in an atmosphere of restrained but defiant celebration. Three luminous pathways, where Hotere has ground the porous, charred surface of the boat's timber back to the heartwood, converge at the centre of the installation. While the floor section, like a wooden jetty or a vessel's wake in a dark sea, calls the viewer forward, the massed vertical elements form a protective phalanx, a shadowy echo of the walls of a fortified pa. The tacit presence of this structure reinforces the suggestion that *Black Phoenix* alludes to the fate of Hotere's Te Aupouri tribe, reputed to have set their pa on fire to escape their enemies, eluding capture in the resulting smoke and then rising again from the ashes like the legendary phoenix. The broader metaphor, of a people threatened, evicted but undeterred, is one with undiminished relevance for life in post-colonial Aotearoa.

Aramoana (1982, see previous page) extends Hotere's use of corrugated iron as the basis for a defensive structure. Ten battered, speckled and inscribed panels hang together staunchly from a horizontal wooden support, the gaps between them looming out like the posts of a white palisade fence. The rusty iron panels make unexpectedly compelling

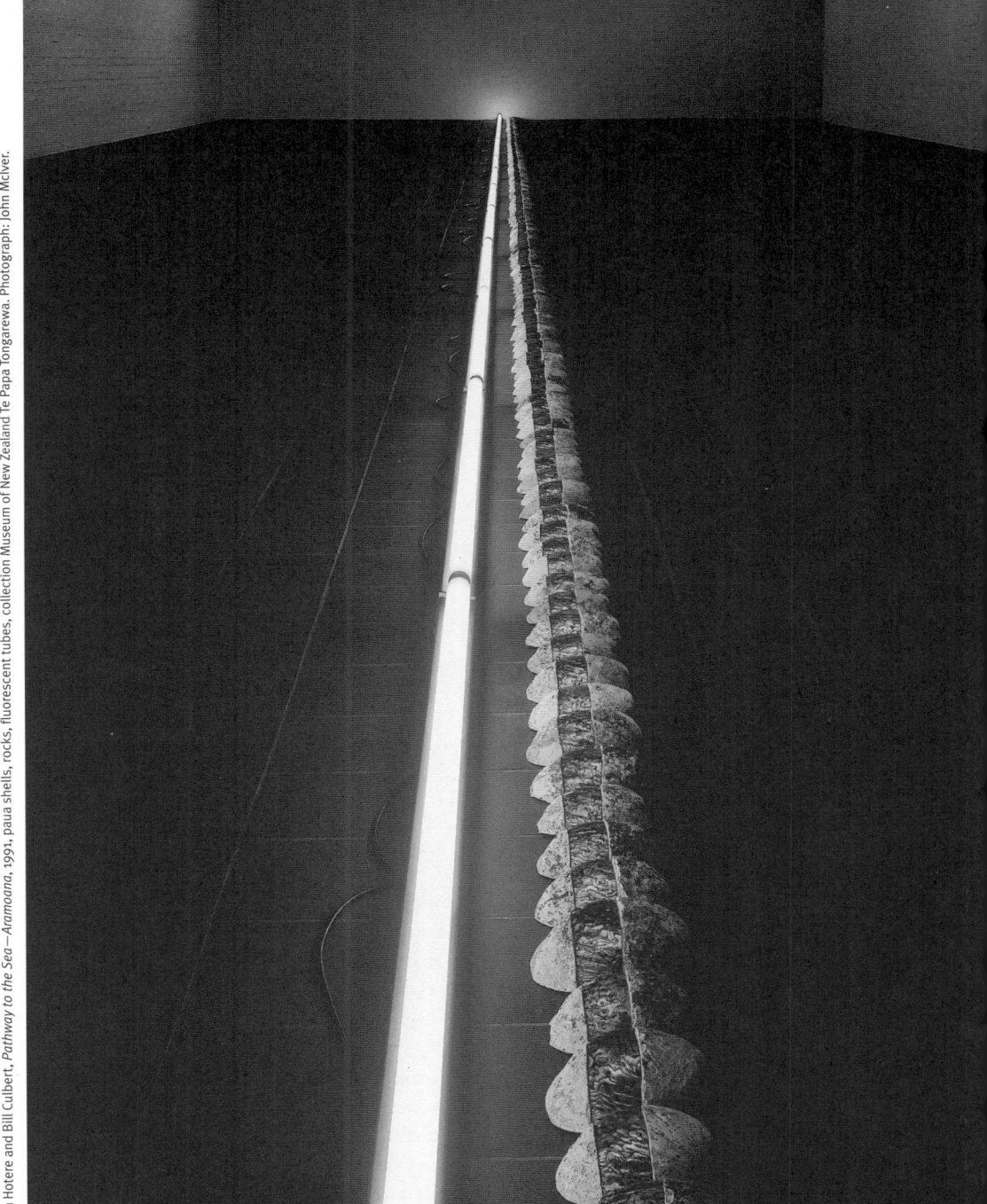

Ralph Hotere and Bill Culbert, *Pathway to the Sea—Aramoana*, 1991, paua shells, rocks, fluorescent tubes, collection Museum of New Zealand Te Papa Tongarewa. Photograph: John McIver.

banners of protest, an honest and eloquent rebuttal of the proposal, ultimately abandoned, to build an aluminium smelter near the Aramoana township, at the mouth of the Otago Harbour, thus threatening the delicate tidal flats and local albatross colony. The word ARAMOANA, stencilled at the top of each sheet like a location marker on a line of railway carriages, gains momentum across the work, culminating in a note of triumphant exclamation: VIVE ARAMOANA. Running down the dull furrows of the iron, narrow streams of milky (and occasionally ox-blood) paint resemble the swift fall of water from rain clouds into the frothing surf. If read from above, however, these shapes repeat the distinctively undeviating form of the mole at Aramoana, a structure designed to protect the inner harbour from the build-up of silt.

The notion of the corrugated surface as a defensive barrier is further evolved in later works such as *Black Cerulean* (1999), in which the black structure is peeled back to reveal a shallow horizontal slit, reminiscent of the narrow window of a fortified parapet or the sinister eye holes of renegade Ned Kelly's crudely fashioned outlaw helmet. In their combination of the refined and the robust, such works seem to distil the tradition in New Zealand architecture that David Mitchell called 'The Elegant Shed', while reminding us that the shed can also be a place of refuge—a shelter, a bunker, a hideout. Hotere is famous for his wily defiance of local body building codes, and his work, with its refusal to stay within genre boundaries, could itself be regarded as a subtle transgression of the 'building codes' for both sculpture and painting.

In *Pathway to the Sea—Aramoana* (1991, see previous page) Culbert and Hotere use metaphors of structure to bring home the potential fragility of nature. A line of hull-like paua shells, flanked and illuminated by Culbert's fluorescent pipeline, again recalls the form of the Aramoana mole, a needle-straight breakwater constructed between 1884 and 1926 from submerged boulders and the hulks of wrecked ships. The dull, overturned shells, each with its centre section ground down to reveal the translucent blue gleam of polished nacre, seem to suggest the new role of these sunken ships, long unfit for service, and subsequently, the possibilities for the redemption and redeployment of even the most damaged goods. As the mole shelters the harbour, so each shell offers not only its own small act of protection but also a supporting pathway over which to move forward. (This is why the installation of this work in Te Papa—on a gimmicky catwalk that literally backed the work into a corner—seemed especially heavy-handed.)

Hotere's architectural impulses attain their zenith in his use of reflection to create a space that allows the viewer to enter his work. As Michelangelo Pistoletto painted on mirrors in the early '60s in an attempt to connect the painted subject with the world in which it exists, so Hotere uses mirrors and mirror-like surfaces to challenge the intellectual and physical divisions between art and the living world. The mirror creates a space that is at once positive and negative, an environment inhabited, and altered, by its audience. The spectator's presence, and thus their transformation of the surface, infects the work with the forms and atmosphere of its surroundings.

When the deep black surface of Blackwater seems as empty as death, the viewer merely has to walk around it for their reflection and shifting gaze to create the impression of movement, of light and life. It seems appropriately perverse that in this work, which takes its name from the legendary primeval blackness of a West Coast lake, corrugated iron should finally resemble roofing. It is not the iron itself which projects this possibility, but rather the triangulations of light-shadows cast by the upright fluorescent tubes, which appear to lift up corners of the metal in a series of sharply pointed peaks. These shapes shift, collapse and re-form as you walk around the work, leaving the lasting impression of a seemingly simple surface within, out of which unfolds a limitless universe, visible only in glances. In this way, perhaps, Blackwater reflects the faith underpinning all of Hotere's building sites—that a definitive, final meaning will prove elusive, but the invitation to enter, and the means to do so, is always, generously, there.

GREGORY O'BRIEN

Rocks, Te Namu Pa, Taranaki

I have seen the tribe upstanding
as waves of a sea and I have seen them

collapse, from the inside
like tents, their poles removed, or as trees

flattened on a hillside. Because there were
people here once, not just stones

long conversations wading the river, then lingering
as the light that lingers on its bed

of evening boulders, isolated clouds
nestled around the mountain

and tomorrow's rain as it falls,
as it is supposed to fall.

Untitled

Water, you are unwell
a stone falls through
your battered embrace

like the heaviest
weather or a comet plummeting
through space. If you had

daughters they would be
a line of markers
in the harbour

of your body, not at all far
from the entrance, signalling
the channel out.

A Modern Colonial

'In my search for the Rainbow's end, I found not gold but this house instead. If you are in search of your Rainbow's end then look no more my friend as this property hides both ends.' (*Harcourts Bluebook*, October 1995)

Make me yours, in fabulous Oriental Bay. Where boats
go by, dreams come true. Relax, put your feet

up. How many square
feet? There is no comparison. With such

excellent sun, minimum garden, Rather A Pretty American
Colonial. Then *Give Me Some Style*

just add awnings, clay tiles and hey presto:
Style! You want three bedrooms, modern kitchen

redecorated bathroom, you got it. Views to
behold. Spacious is the word, 'beauty in the bush'.

A must. *Hey look me over!* Design your own
dream. You'd look lovely in low

maintenance, a corner in time, and like these
several fruit trees, would respond well

to the personal touch—sun, wonderful returns
drop dead views. At last we have a waterfront

property for you, with everything
you need and possibly more.

'Wanted—A Family To Own Me.'
Always phone Paulane.

Cowgirl in the Sand

Jane Gardner

It's the woman in you that makes you want to play this game . . .

Merv knocked at eight-fifteen on a Monday morning. Rooster had shot down the drive in the Hillman about seven-forty-five. The door was painted what used to be called 'old rose'. A muddy, brickish colour, peeling through to grey.

Merv said he wasn't stopping, he'd be late for taking his class on an outing, but he wanted me to listen to his new tape and give it back later in the week. Just like that. I'd only met the man once. There was nothing shy about him. He was confident, almost intense in the way he looked at me as he gave me the tape. Neil Young's *Harvest*. Lyrics: mostly about forms of loneliness and frustration; music: jumpy, haunted. I hadn't heard it before either, not that Merv would have known.

I played music all day long then, as you do when you're young. We'd bought an old, hard roll-arm sofa to furnish the living room. I'd made some cushions to go on it, out of stripy Indian cotton, blue and red, which niggled with yellowed, grey moquette from the '20s. Little Bob and I sat there, even though it was Monday, listening to Neil asking us to see the lonely boy out on the weekend. Straight across the road, the view was of Williams the retired railway worker, mowing his front lawn to dust in front of his yellowed grey state house so it would be tidy before the bloke from the hotel delivered the crate of flagons. He mowed it most days. His house was incredibly clean inside, thanks to Mrs Williams, but everything smelled of beer, even the water in the toilet cistern.

We had nothing much in the way of furniture, but we did have stereo speakers the size of phone boxes, built by Rooster. The neighbour through the wall of the semi-detached worked during the day so there was nobody to complain about Neil's force-ten wailing. I thought that Merv must be a bit in love with me the way he'd lent me the tape like that. I was totally riveted by *Harvest* and Bob and the unborn baby rocked to its rhythms.

Merv and family had only recently moved in down the road. We were fairly new to the place too. Neil Young was insistent that a man needs a maid, but Merv had Peg after all, even if they did say nasty things to each other in public, public being us who they'd never met before saying hi and them inviting us in for a cup of tea. Merv had mentioned that he was a Freudian, and believed that saying what he thought made for better relationships. Rooster found this boring and/or embarrassing. I was fascinated. Maybe Merv knew something I didn't about the human condition. I could learn about such things while I was getting through life the best I could. This was my full-time attitude then. This was what actually started me reading books on psychology from the library. I don't recall returning the tape, which is strange, all things considered. It was replaced by an LP, one of many featuring Neil, which I still have.

Mrs Williams had given us an old armchair with torn red vinyl upholstery, and offered to help babysit Bob when the new baby came. Her false teeth gleamed in a kind smile, her wrinkles deep enough for crumbs to rest in. Bob liked her, but I was put off by all the beeriness, and made an excuse. I wanted only the chair. Bob sat in it, reading a library book upside down. Being the person he was, he virtually ignored Jude for about three months after he was born, quietly consumed with jealousy on the one hand, and taking his lead from Rooster on the other. Rooster was interested in women's liberation and was often away, especially in the weekend, though he didn't seem anything like the lonely boy. He just wanted a tolerant marriage and definitely more sex in his life than he was having with me.

Somewhere in the fairly sleepless chaos of my life with a disapproving toddler and a new baby Merv rang me from his school about four o'clock in the afternoon. Rooster drove from Wellington and was never home much before six.

'I want to tell you because I know you'll understand,' said Merv. 'You know I'm doing guidance counselling?' I'd shown great interest in the content of Merv's extra courses of study but still felt that his wisdom was arcane. I was respectful of his extra decade of life and impressed by a fine scar which ran from under his right ear lobe, traced his jawbone toward his chin, and leaped up sharply to plunge into his lower lip where it swelled from the corner of his mouth. I wouldn't have dared to ask him how he got this mark of endurance any more than I would have wondered out loud why he only ever wore shorts. He told me that a girl at the college had fallen in love with one of her teachers.

'A great problem. Do you know how I got her to fall out of love with him?' The telephone was on the wall behind the front door. My face was reflected dully in the doorknob, one of those oval brass ones where the crystals of the metal show on the surface from the constant action of human sweat. I looked like a mosaic half-buried in sand.

'How?'

'By making her fall in love with me.'

I blurted, how had he done that? I thought perhaps with a certain glance of his blue eyes. He laughed softly at the question. Things hadn't had time to progress to the point of putting the girl off Merv, curing her of inappropriate loves forever. She'd thrown herself under a train, he told me. He couldn't help wondering if he'd mismanaged things, though it was a fact that she'd had problems for a very long time.

'I'm sure you did your best,' murmured the mosaic, sand falling into its tiny mouth.

'This is just between you and me,' said Merv. 'I'm not sharing about it with anyone else. By the way, could you babysit Max tonight so Peg and I can go to a Pre-school meeting?'

Max was older than Bob and Jude and smelled of pee. I couldn't recognise either of his parents' features in his pointy little face except for Merv's wide eyes. Max's eyes were narrowed when he looked at me. He had hundreds of Matchbox cars, among other things, that I envied for my children. Peg was a qualified physio and had a part-time job, so they could afford lots of toys. They were lying in heaps all over the room, which was open-plan and yellow. Merv proudly showed me a complex motorway he had built with blocks for Max to drive the cars on.

What Peg and I had in common was that we were the only women in Waitone to be wearing long dresses in the early '70s, but of course we were recent arrivals there, sophisticated imports. The indigenous female population was still in the mini. Rooster and I had come there only because we couldn't afford to live in Wellington. Travelling by train with two small children to visit friends in town was becoming more and more difficult for me. The children got overtired being out all day, and nobody wanted to come out to hoonland to visit me very often, leaving their shabby colonial houses with romantic overgrown gardens in Northland or Glenmore Street. Their cars were in for servicing or were out of petrol. Our state flat was clean but bleak. It looked out on other state houses, on flatness barely relieved by distant gorse-covered hills, on old cars, on a fusty, working-class dormitory.

Peg looked at me with her very black eyes and didn't smile but then she didn't smile at many people. She adored only Merv. She stubbed out a fag in a huge ashtray. I remembered Merv saying they 'used cigarettes after sex'. They weren't constant smokers like Rooster and me. Max hung on and whined and it was late before they left. Max told me he wouldn't do what I told him, that is, go to sleep. I told him I would smack him if he didn't, though I regretted saying it when I actually looked at his scrawny, winceyetted bottom. Merv and Peg didn't babysit for Rooster and me but then Rooster and I never went out together really.

'I'll tell Merv and Peg if you smack me,' said Max.

'You do that, I don't care.' I knew he would tell them anyway. Max was well aware of what was scandalous. 'Now go to sleep.' I wanted to phone Rooster and check on the well-being of Bob and Jude. Maybe the Clays wouldn't ask me to babysit again. Perhaps they would. Peg would hate me with her eyes and say nothing.

I wanted to sort things out with Merv. My admiration for him was a leper's ulcer. I knew he would never leave Peg and I would never leave Rooster, nothing absurd like that. I couldn't imagine how we could have an affair since having an affair was a Rooster-only prerogative in my marriage. Any liking was over between Rooster and me, and so far only strict attention to my responsibilities and interests muffled my unpleasant thoughts. I studied the care of children, the science of stain removal, discovered the combustion of Janola bottles to help dry nappies in winter, worked hard at the manufacture of an elegant family wardrobe from sale remnants and furnishing fabrics, read numberless books, to give but a few examples of my ceaseless activities. One way or another I believed I wasn't giving myself any opportunity for self-indulgence.

Bob started Pre-school when Jude was three months old. That was when I met Lee. Lee had been left by Phil with three kids in a Lockwood house up in the bush. Jojo, her youngest, was Bob's friend. They ran around the shopping centre saying 'poopoos and farties' to people. Jojo took her clothes off, which didn't bother Bob or me, but upset Lee. I told her not to worry about it.

'Don't you think so?' asked Lee, with wide, grateful eyes.

'Of course not,' replied the reader of books, 'she's just expressing her natural self. It's probably a peak experience for her.' (Maslow).

Lee confided that Phil had left her for a woman who looked like a horse. Lee was beautiful like the woman in the paintings by Rossetti. Horseface made no sense. When I met Phil on an occasion when he'd come to visit the children, I saw that he looked like the Rossetti woman too. The polished timbers of the house and the shadows of the tree-ferns falling through the windows set him off to perfection as he sat sipping a cup of tea held delicately between tapered fingers. The children hovered like cobwebs, silent except for Jojo. 'Daddy, Daddy,' she yelled. Phil regarded her, curving his lips, spoke to Lee and me in a husky voice, pushed his black curls from his impossibly fine eyes. No wonder Jojo was so beautiful. No wonder Bob loved her. They danced around our lounge together to the strains of The Beatles' 'Get Back'. *Jojo was a man who thought he was a woman—.* They were three years old, they were naked, they were happy.

Phil told me he was in counselling because of the separation. Lee, he informed me, needed to feel her depression. 'She won't divorce me,' he said, 'it's driving me mad.'

Lee struggled on, trying to bring up the family on nothing much. 'I won't let him go, he's their father,' she repeated in more than one phone call after our children had been put to bed and *Family at War* had finished on TV.

I was relieved that Rooster didn't show too much interest in sleeping with her. She disliked him but was too polite to say so. He said she was an old-fashioned girl, like me. Her bountiful curls were unbrushed and her breasts shrank under her old T-shirt. Lee's thighs in her jeans were pencil thin. Her teeth seemed too large for her face. One evening Phil rang me and told me he had a hose on the exhaust pipe of his car and was about to kill himself.

'Go ahead,' I said, hanging up. Lee rang me the next day. 'He's come back, I've got him back.' When I went there later in the week he was in bed with the door open, where he stayed silently all the time I was there, tracing hieroglyphs on the bedcover with his eloquent hands. Lee and I huddled in the lounge, out of his line of sight. At the end of a fortnight he was gone again, to be cold-turkeyed off his antidepressants in a bin for the unusually privileged.

I was seeing a lot of Merv because of my involvement with Pre-school. We were on the committee together though lately we'd avoided each other's houses. Max had started school and one of the girls from the college babysat him. Peg, working full-time, was finished with Pre-school involvements and Rooster had never begun them. Merv felt it was his civic duty to retain his position as chairman of the parents' committee. He believed Pre-school education was the most important formative experience of a child's life. He lent me books written by far-out Pre-school equivalents of Timothy Leary, gurus from Takaka or the far North. He didn't ask me what I thought of them, although I wanted to tell him. I felt it was my civic duty to catalogue the Pre-school library and write the weekly newsletter, in which I rehashed my newly acquired understanding of child development. The indigenous mothers of Waitone didn't take an interest. Friday, the day the newsletter came out, was the day when the footpath outside Pre-school was covered with drifts of them, dropped by mums who'd come to collect only their Jasons and Lisa-Marees.

After a well-attended fundraising evening at which the main attraction was a demonstration of a famous brand of skin-care and cosmetic products, I asked Merv for a ride home. This was okay, since I couldn't drive. I'd made a new blouse in psychedelic curtaining which went well with flared jeans given to me by an old friend in town. The colours showed up my tan, acquired in the long grass out the back of the house while Bob splashed in the plastic paddling pool. The weight of the sun was the weight of Merv on me. Jude crawling over me, dragging wet nappies, shook me out of the dream.

I'd refrained from smoking all afternoon. My hands shook. Something had to happen now and I didn't know what.

'Can you park, Merv? I need to talk to you.'

'Aaah, sure. I haven't got a lot of time though. How about here?'

'Not right under a bloody street light.' My heart flailed like an angry fist. Merv stiffened and backed up a few yards. 'We don't want anyone to see us having this chat, I suppose,' he said. 'Is something wrong?'

'Please drive up Rua Street, away from here.'

'No. It has to be here.'

Even Waitone has its blue evening hour. Stars come out and sodium lights come on. We were enveloped in the summer dusk. There was peace and cicada song, a sense of time out.

'I love you, Merv.'

'I know that.' He sat with his face averted. His skin looked grey and shiny. 'What I don't know is what you want me to do about it. There is nothing to be done.'

What did I babble next? All my plans, perhaps, too awful, crazy, shameful to remember, all the plans I didn't know I had. To say I surprised myself is . . . well, there has to be a first time. Merv said nothing. No thing. I unfastened my seat belt.

'Undo your seat belt, please Merv.' He shook his head, so I undid it for him but he sat there as though tied up with rope. 'Nothing can happen between us,' he said, slamming his foot on the brake.

'At least let me kiss you. Please let me have that.' He stared silently out at the dark road. I could feel the blood beating in my breasts. He'd watched me so many times, lips parted and wet, as I nursed Jude. Had Peg fed Max? I forced my kiss on his mouth. His mouth stayed still, dry as a stone.

So I opened the car door and walked away. If I thought of anything at all, it was that I understood why Phil might once have wanted to die.

Lee started up from her kitchen table as I came in with Bob and Jude. Her eyes were red and her face streaked. She put her arms out to me as my children rushed towards Jojo, smiling around the door of the lounge. Jude could rush on all fours if a party was on.

In the lounge, the tape deck clicked and music poured through the house like smoke. There were giggles and the stomp of dancing feet. *If a picture paints a thousand words* . . . 'Baa baa baa!' roared Jude. Lee and I hugged and she sniffled into my shoulder.

'Where have you been for a whole month?' she said. 'I've missed you.'

'You're crying. I don't think I've seen you cry before. Dear Lee.'

'I'm divorcing Phil. I'm going to let him have the divorce. When I didn't hear from you for a while I thought you didn't want to know about my troubles any more.' I had been the one who phoned most often. 'I rang and rang. I nearly rang Rooster at work. I'm so glad you rang me.' Having dazed me with this ringing speech, the usually taciturn Lee made tea. I offered reassurances and we sat down together. 'What have you been doing?' she said.

'Having an affair with Merv Clay.'

'What?' Lee knocked over her mug and we scrambled to restore order with a Wettex and the teapot. 'Does Peg know?'

'No, I'm pretty sure she doesn't.'

'That's a relief! I hate Peg anyway, don't you? Don't you think she's got deep, dark depths you don't want to know about?' Lee had been getting in touch with her psychological theories too. 'What's going to happen?' I definitely had her attention. Her eyes, radiant with beauty and pain, held mine.

'I don't know—well, nothing, I think,' I said. 'I don't love him.'

Lee could quickly grasp this great swathe of experience, taking it in her stride, even adding her own resonances. Dear Lee. How knowledgeable we were now.

'Tell me how it happened.'

'He came in one day when Rooster was away. He told me he wanted me. He kissed me. We took it from there.'

'Where were the boys?' asked the ever-practical Lee.

'Asleep,' I said.

BERNADETTE HALL

Shelter Belt

Native or exotic?
Hey, you calling me exotic?

Crossed the Rakaia,
heading down to Ash-Vegas,
drifting past Nifty Gifts, Home World, Waterloo
Wreckers, the Top Hat Café, Hamilton jet,
the usual spring stock losses.

I stayed a day and a night in Austria.
I wasn't impressed.

Ah, the hauteur of the may tree,
chocolate rough, sweet serein,
a cockatoo hanging upside down
over the front entrance to The Warehouse.

Want to get into security?
Get a gun licence.

Your car clicking when you turn it on?

Do yourself a favour
            and become a Christain.

Do yourself a favour
            and learn how to spell.

Open Field

The earth's cold sweat, white rime on the rectangular
field like beds of daisies, the moisture cool on your arms
like ointment and on your face; the trees standing around
patient as pack-horses; the blue militia, the white hikoi.

Standing out in the open field, you slow your breathing,
you go deeper, blue swishes on the white sky, smooth
as the stone the little black poodle places on the polished
floor for you to throw thrillingly beyond her obsession.

The trees are heavy with green cloud, a tent you can walk
under and the light changes. You're taller, your skin opens
with little pricking sounds, up and down the airy ladder
the plucking of soft nests, like Chris's aeolian harp.

We are what we love and you love the way the painter fades
the body into the page so the paper itself becomes the skin.
The way she opens the head as you might a field cleanly
with a spade, the sea streaming sideways like a Ugandan postmark.

Underwood

Saskia Leek

KATE CAMP

Old West Miniature Town

Only one of the inhabitants is pure
evil. Not unfeeling he feels as the blind
read—with his hands. On the back of God
only knows what kind of horse he comes.
The dust puffs, dogs lose their senses.
Even the air is trembling.

Shuttered in the saloon is one sad piano
leaning woman. There are packets of matches
all around her and something she doesn't care
to forgive easing itself into a low, leather chair.

There's a train depot, but the train is not included.
There's a water tower, but it has never known water.
There is nothing keeping this town alive.

Between the outhouse and the woodhouse
the woodhouse and the outhouse is a figure.
Some believe him the sheriff, see a star on him,
others say he is just a Jew, lost in the wrong box.
The figure never shoots anyone so it's hard to tell if he is real
ly one of the good guys.

The hero of the miniature Old West town
goes by the name of Jig. He comes to the door without
music. In his hands are papers he serves
undressed. 'I can save you
money' they say. 'I will help you
switch.' He inherited his eyes from a faithful
pet who never thought to meet death at your hand.
He comes from India. He comes from where you dare not travel.

RHYS WILLIAMSON

Or We Could Talk About the Weather

Late in the afternoon a creeping silence rolls down off the hills, sweeping across the valley, over the feet of the dancing librarians. The librarians dance around a bonfire of old wives' tales and young men's conceits. They dance with flair and abandon. They dance late into the night. They dance by the light of the silvery moon. By the morning the librarians have turned into stone bookends.

'Yes, this is how I remember it,' said Kate, stepping out of the car and looking out over the mute landscape. 'Hostile. Unkempt. Savage. A luxurious sprawl of earth and sky and scrubby vegetation, and yes, that distinctive odour—I can smell marshmallow. Nature,' said Kate, 'is the armpit of God.'

'I like it,' said Bob. 'The feel of it. The touch of it. Nature. The warmth of the sun. The soft caress of the wind. The abundance of natural sounds. The air. The clarity of light. Nature,' said Bob, 'is a multimedia extravaganza—a whipping wind, pipes and drums, light from a distant star.'

'Couldn't agree more,' said Tony. 'It's quietly stimulating. The big sky. The wide-eyed fields. The studious trees. Nature,' said Tony, 'is the default background to the rich tapestry of life.'

'When we part,' said the girl, 'and I murder you in my heart, I will take my loss to a mean and selfish man and offer him, without conditions, his fill of my smoky kisses and his way with my body, my body as grey as ashes. He will except the offer, as his due, and only say: "You should take better care of yourself." Later, after he is done, he will fall asleep and I will watch him through eyes as cold as the moon. Involuntarily he will shudder in his sleep and I will turn and let him be. He will wake in the morning and go without waking me, but he will not leave, not until he has carefully checked each of his pockets; searching them for rain.'

'In the country,' suggested Kate, 'there are few distractions but the weather. Brooding black clouds bellying out across the landscape. The wretched wind snaking down the road. A menacing darkness spreading under the trees. I believe there are some late nineteenth century novels that are completely indebted to the weather for their plot and structure, all of which are artfully translated into the emotions of a few characterless peasants. Art as a weather-cock!'

'Before the advent of the twentieth century,' said Bob, 'the contemplation of Nature was an accepted part of everyday life. It was natural for people to take time each day to reflect on Nature and their part in it. Today the natural world is seen as being somewhat twee.'

'Nature as a Theme Park,' said Tony.

'To the astonishment of many and to the delight of a few, she came to the ceremony wearing nothing but a cloud,' commented Kate.

'At the same time,' continued Bob, 'bolstered by a growing army of sympathetic supporters, Nature is coming again. It's back there on the billboards. It's up there on the screen. They are singing about it. They are wearing it.'

'Yes,' said Kate. 'The birds are returning to the forest, but where have they been?'

'When we part,' he said, 'I will cleave to the wind, to hurl myself against tree and barn, expending my fury like a navvy his wages. The wind will humour me like a flag, then without warning it will unceremoniously drop me into the vacuum of your heart and its ambiguous silence.'

'Nature,' said Kate, 'is a hypothesis of Creation.'

Finding himself on the same side of the road as the weather, the weather approaching fast from the opposite direction, the young man slipped into a covered doorway with the intention of waiting until the bad weather had passed. The bad weather passed by, dragging its feet. Tied to each ankle was a string of empty cans. The weather was smoking like the rain.

But there was still no sign of rain in Fairfield. It hadn't rained for over six months now and everything and everyone had suffered as a result. Nevertheless, the town of Fairfield continued to go about its business, albeit slowly, like an arthritic gigolo, polite and caring as always but a little edgy. Above Fairfield the glorious sun was ever shining, bound fast to the shimmering blue sky—bound to the body of the sky as the golden chain and pendant was bound to the body of the ageing, arthritic gigolo. Was there nothing to be done then—nothing left to do, that is, in the town of Fairfield; for the people of Fairfield had not been idle. They had applied themselves to the water crisis with a single-minded determination, not unlike that of the labouring, arthritic, gigolo . . .

She jumped, jumped out of the plane. I can't describe how she must have felt, only imagine. Like throwing the garbage out and you are the garbage, only now you are something else, or perhaps for that one sweet moment nothing at all; and we down below, standing on the ground waiting, staunch as trees, nursing the weather.

'I imagine,' said Kate, 'there are towns; towns that are dependent on the cooperation of the weather for their survival, where the mayor is still seen as an intermediary between the needs of the community and the vagaries of Nature. An overweight shaman in robes and chain. Never short of something to say.'
    'Like a rooster with weather stuck up his arse,' said Bob.
    'In the square,' said Tony, 'a crowd awaits the arrival of the mayor and civic party. They gaze up at the town clock, slow as any sun. The people expect some kind of initiative as they expect rain. A jazz band plays.'

We killed a cock and hung it up on the weather. We drew smoke from a mirror and it tightened into rain. With sharpened knives we bled a riverbed. With insults and loud cries we worried the sky. We stuffed ashes into a snake's hide. With a multicoloured kite we dredged the sky. We sprinkled salt on our dusty wives. We called the rainmaker.

The rainmaker came to town. He was carrying a dead donkey. Bending under its weight, he made his way to the town square. In the square he looked about him at the shuffling crowds, the disconsolate faces. 'I am the Gatherer of Fields,' he proclaimed. A scruffy looking bird alighted on the dead donkey, still shouldered by the rainmaker, and began pecking vigorously at the carcass. The rainmaker dropped the carcass to the ground. One or two people, a few, and then a crowd gathered around the rainmaker. He addressed the crowd: 'Paradise has turned sour,' he said. 'The sun is a dry biscuit. The little brook a weeping memory. Birds infest the sky. They darken it with desire. The machinery of faith is broken and rusting at the bottom of the garden. There is despair in the factory. Tears in the classroom. There is a serpent nesting on the wind.'

It was Sunday afternoon and we had an audience with the weather. Following lunch we drove to the beach. Everything about the beach I loved, excepting perhaps the seagulls; stringy, beady-eyed scavengers, beach rats, hungry as dogs, bitchy as siblings. But, like a signpost in Paradise, could be overlooked. The weather filtered all extraneous noise. In the Great Hall of Summer we were excused to go and play.

Or perhaps we would drive out into the country. Away from the vast silence and mystery of sea and sky, to the more confined, labyrinthine, patchwork landscape of forest and field. In the bush we would stalk and then capture the elusive sun using only the filigree netting of leaf and light. Or, after a picnic on an unfurnished field, we would run hand in hand with the weather.

It was a spectacular sunrise. The sky was lit up like a baboon's backside. Cerise, red, orange—a hundred different hues; crimson, vermilion—all of them brilliant. We were spellbound. We were talking underwater; looking for the right words, for an expression that would give us a handle on this wondrous spectacle: Gay as a car-yard; a coloured cartoon; a fire in Chinatown; a pirate tale . . .

And then it was gone; all the colour drained from the sky: 'O! where shall I my true-love find?'

'I can appreciate a good sunset as much as the next man,' said the rainmaker. 'It is not all business, you know. I am not Nature's whore.'

'It is evening,' said Kate, 'the world is on tilt. The birds are in the trees, whistling—ad libbing. We are off on a walk. Nature is movement, change. I feel I am being undermined by my own good sense.'

'Kate,' said Bob, 'you are an inspiration to us all. Magnificent as the soft battle of dawn.'

'There are trees in my history,' said Kate. 'There are mornings I remember. There is water in subterranean passes. There are cliffs at twilight. If you were to help me; my memory needs turning like a compost.'

'We want our fair-weather coupons,' demanded the disenchanted, queuing up along the railway lines. 'We want our hearts weighed. We want credit for our anger.' There were cans and wrappers strewn along the length of the railway line. There were mothers and babies piled up like driftwood. 'We want a tax on freedom,' they said. 'A tax on faith.' Scrubby brush clung tenaciously to the railway sidings. A railway hoarding battered with rocks was broken in places, holed in others. 'We want a refund on lost enjoyment. We want those wearing yellow or red to pay.' But the line was breaking. They were leaving. Peeling off the railway tracks. Stalking off across the fields. Grey figures in a grey landscape. Coming to a town near you soon—the community of rain. 'But mostly,' they spat out as they filed away, 'we want nothing; especially from you!'

'You have your doubts,' suggested the rainmaker. 'You are sceptical but because of the seriousness of your situation, you are also vulnerable. And I can't say I blame you, you have my sympathy; but let me tell you this, a rainmaker is only as good as his last thunderstorm and mine was a ripper.' Here the rainmaker kicked the dead donkey. 'No doubt you would like some kind of explanation, a short demonstration, a thunderbolt or two, a little something to take home with you to set your minds at rest—I can't do that. I am not a street performer. Not any sort of performer at all really, come to think of it. I was only being facetious when I boasted of my thunderstorm. I like to think of rainmaking as nothing more grand than a simple cottage industry. And now, I'm sorry, I must go and find myself a room and then bury my burrow.'

'And what do you do in a town like this,' said Kate, 'after you have called
Nature's bluff? After you have closed the book with its yellowing, dog-eared
fields? And there above the hill, the frayed edges of the sky where the
rainmaker has been scratching himself. And the sun, kind enough on its day,
become terrible in a malevolent sky. And Fairfield nothing but a skin hung to
dry along the fence line. Tell me what do you do?' said Kate.

    'Box on,' said Bob.

Every time it rained the house shrank. For twenty years he had been running
on the spot. He felt like a poodle in a car wash. He looked like the History of
the World in paperback. So he built himself a teepee. Tacked it to a hill. A
house for the weather and its bastard brood. Nights after work he sat in the
teepee. Sat cross-legged on a blanket. Released his mind and his hands. It
was more than a gesture—a flag in the rain. A statement—I am not your
ordinary head-banging goldfish dear! It was a celebration—watch this blow!
In the kitchen his yeasty wife grew more livid by the minute. Although
occupied, busy preparing tea or the like, she couldn't help herself. Every few
moments her concentration would fail, her attention stray, and she would be
looking out the window, up the hill to where he sat in his teepee—a garden
gnome in buckskin.

Outside the window there came a pathetic cry: the sound of the sun pinching
the sky.

'And don't come creeping around here—creeping around here like the
weather.'

The rainmaker had been in town a week and there was still no change in the
weather. 'I am a facilitator,' said the rainmaker when pressed, 'not a purge.'
This didn't help the people of Fairfield. They were anxious. If the rainmaker
failed them too, what were their remaining options? 'You must continue to
have faith,' said the rainmaker. 'Faith is a wheel. Faith is a shiny sixpence.
Faith is concrete. Faith is vertigo. Faith is a dead burrow. Let's see: We could
talk about the weather. The weather now. The weather then. You and the
weather. Or we could wait. Don't you think the flowers smell sweeter this

morning than they did yesterday?'

Early morning. Black trees. Grey sky. A whisper of wind. Standing in a field of abandoned car wrecks, the rainmaker urinates on the ground. A gesture of resignation, defeat? Or was it? By mid-morning the wind is blowing fresh. The sky is busy with gathering clouds. Also congregating, the people of Fairfield hold their breath.

MARGARET ATWOOD

Questioning the Dead

Go to the mouth of a cave,
dig a trench, slit the throat
of an animal, pour out the blood.

Or sit in a chair
with others, at a round table
in a darkened room.
Close your eyes, hold hands.

These techniques might be called
the heroic and the mezzotint.
We aren't sure we believe in either,

or in the dead, when they do appear,
smelling like damp hair,
flickering like faulty toasters,
rustling their tissue paper
faces, their sibilants, their fissures,
trailing their fraudulent gauze.

Their voices are dry as lentils
falling into a glass jar.
Why can't they speak up clearly
instead of mumbling about keys and numbers,
and stairs, they mention stairs . . .

Why do we keep pestering them?
Why do we insist they love us?
What did we want to ask them
anyway? Nothing they wish to tell.

Or stand by a well or pool
and drop in a pebble.
The sound you hear is the question
you should have asked.

Also the answer.

Sor Juana Works in the Garden

Time for gardening again; for poetry; for arms
up to the elbows in leftover
deluge, hands in the dirt, groping around
among the rootlets, bulbs, lost marbles, blind
snouts of worms, cat droppings, your own future
bones, whatever's down there
supercharged, a dim glint in the darkness.
When you stand on bare earth in your bare feet
and the lightning whips through you, two ways
at once, they say you are grounded,
and that's what poetry is: a hot wire.
You might as well stick a fork
in a wall socket. So don't think it's just about flowers.
Though it is, in a way.
You spent this morning among the bloodsucking
perennials, the billowing peonies,
the lilies building to outburst,
the leaves of the foxgloves gleaming like hammered
copper, the static crackling among the spiny columbines.
Scissors, portentous trowel, the wheelbarrow
yellow and inert, the grass-blades
whispering like ions. You think it wasn't all working

up to something? You ought to have worn rubber
gloves. Thunder budding in the spires of lupins,
their clumps and updrafts, pollen and resurrection
unfolding from each restless nest
of petals. Your arms hum, the hair
stands up on them; just one touch and you're struck.
It's too late now, the earth splits open,
the dead rise, purblind and stumbling
in the clashing of last-day daily
sunlight, furred angels crawl
all over you like swarming bees, the maple
trees above you shed their deafening keys
to heaven, your exploding
syllables litter the lawn.

Crickets

September. Wild aster. Fox grapes,
tiny and bitter,
the indigo taste of winter
already blooming inside them.

The house is invaded by crickets,
they've come inside for the warmth.
They creep into the stove
and behind the refrigerator,
make sorties across the floor,
singing to one another:
Here, here, here, here.
We step on them by mistake,
or pick them up, dozens of them,

dozens of wriggling black consciences
and throw them out the door.

There's nothing for them to eat,
not with us. No more harvests or granaries,
only tables and chairs.
We have become too affluent.
Inside, they'd die of hunger.
Wait, wait, wait, wait, they say. They fear
they'll freeze. Under the broom
their dark armour crackles.

The ant and the grasshopper have
their places in our bestiaries:
the first stows wealth, the second
spends. We hold the middle ground, approve
the ant (head), love
the (heart) grasshopper,
emulate both: why choose?
We hoard and fiddle.

As for the crickets, they've
been censored. We have
no crickets on our hearths. We have no hearths.

Nevertheless, they wake
us at cold midnight,
small timid voices we can't locate,
small watches ticking away,
cheap ones; small tin mementos:
late, late, late, late,
somewhere in the bedsheets,
in the bedsprings, in the ear,
the hordes of the starved dead
come back as our heartbeats.

EMMA NEALE

Touchpapers:
The Poetics of the House Fire

I

There are some stories we are compelled to retell as touchstones—or touchpapers—of experience: events that have set alight a change of view or circumstance. Some occurrences break so extraordinarily with our standard perceptions that this in itself offers impetus to frame them in language. These are what the American poet Louise Glück calls 'charged stories or referents, the sorts of stories we tell those [attractive strangers] we wish to befriend, so that they will see what has formed us.'[1]

One such shock to my own assumptions as a twenty-something happened one Friday night, during a freezing English March. It was a night of standing out on the sleety pavement, dressed in a thin cotton nightdress shoved hastily into jeans: feeling a brief scrape from the cold, leathery wings of homelessness, as a fire took hold of the three-storey house my husband and I shared with several others.

Deviating from their routine beat, police had driven down our road, and seen a car they thought was kerb crawling. The occupant, who turned out be a minicab driver, was

calling the fire brigade from his cell phone; he'd seen black rolls of smoke funnelling from one of the second storey rooms.

The sound of police battering down our front door began the most frightening and surreal night I've ever experienced. It, indeed, is one of those accounts I have told and retold to friends and 'attractive strangers'. As it is also one of those events that fractured familiar patterns, and even cherished beliefs, the impulse to write about it has been strong. Yet the power of the impulse has faded even as the lines were written—picture a match, self-consuming, becoming an ashen, ineffectual skeleton. I've never been able to make the events undergo the alterations they must if they were to achieve the state of poetry. As a result, when I've come across poems about house fires, I've leaned in as close as possible, listening for knowledge of what went on in others' burning rooms—and perhaps, by extension, for what went on in my own.

II

The house fire is often a metaphor for material loss, but eventual emotional gain. (An exception is that haunting, taunting childhood rhyme: 'Ladybird, Ladybird, fly away home, your house is on fire, your children are gone.' Or, in one version, 'burned'.) In their various treatments of a house fire, three contemporary women poets—Louise Glück, Margaret Atwood and Cilla McQueen—all, at some level, seek to work out such a balance of ruin and relief. I bring these writers together here not as a scholar tracing literary history, seeking origins or influence—the creative spark passed between poets in a literary Olympiad—but as a reader seeking someone else's words to articulate a profoundly rocking experience. And as a way to try to figure out why that London house fire has always failed, so far, to ignite its own poetry.

If poetry is illumination and transformation, the house fire and the poem seem immediately akin. What is fire, if not light and heat and the process of change? This kinship does appear very early in the world's spiritual and literary history: one ancient source is the 'Parable of the Burning House', which appears in *The Lotus Sutra*, an instructional text based on the teachings of Buddha, who lived roughly 2,500 years ago. The setting for this parable is a rich man's home which is engulfed by flames, while the wealthy father's tiny sons play inside, unaware that the house is burning. Even when the father warns them, they are unable to understand what danger they're in. The father must invent 'expedient means' to rescue them; he tells them that wonderful toys—goat, deer and ox carts—are beyond the gates. Each son, 'emboldened in his heart', rushes outside to safety. The Buddha goes on to say that

There is no safety in the threefold world; it is like a burning house [. . .]

constantly beset with griefs and pains of birth, old age, sickness and death, which are like the fires raging without cease.[2]

Living itself is the inferno: all mortals are trapped in the conflagration of themselves, and ignorant of how they burn. Our attachments to worldly things are the cause of all our suffering.

On a literal level, certainly, a house fire threatens to obliterate worldly goods. These goods can be the symbolic repositories of our very identities, the vessels of our beliefs and values. Additionally, gifts or photos become aide-mémoires, calling up whenever we hold or look at them the memory of this person, of that time . . . For a person who writes, 'worldly goods' can also include manuscripts, and, now, computers. For a writer, that pale-grey plastic box on the desk can be a container of identities, values, memories; a storehouse for years of work; a surrogate home for lives and livelihoods.

As I watched firemen in reflective jackets press towards our building, like creatures drawn to brilliant light who then struggle back from the heat, the realisation slowly dawned. Under a ceiling that was fast drinking in gulps of fire sat my notes, my books, the hard evidence of two years spent writing a Ph.D. thesis. Yet the thought was very slow to come, arriving long after all the tenants were safely on the street (and warmly dressed in the ski-gear my husband had grabbed as he left the building). And now I wonder. Was this delayed reaction just another form of shock, or was an unconscious gamble taking place? Writing a thesis is rarely enjoyable, no matter how strong the compulsion is. In the proximity of the flames to my laptop was there a perverse promise of release? This is the paradoxical lure of the house fire: its power both to destroy and to liberate. It is a fantasy especially potent in a culture like ours, with its fervent belief in ownership, its faith that things help to anchor us. Fire might burn away that weight of possession and leave us lighter than air.

III

Centuries, continents and a cultural divide separate the Buddhist parable from Louise Glück's 'Night Song', first collected in 1985.[3] In her essay 'The Dreamer and the Watcher', Glück cites the poem as an example of the turn her work took after a devastating house fire. My own diary entries shortly after the London incident gnaw over one anxiety: that poetry seems to have stopped. The entries keep connecting this to the blaze, but can't express why the two should be linked. In the wake of her loss Glück discovered the opposite. After the initial silence of crisis, she attained such fluency that she feared she was about to die: the productivity felt unnatural, and, therefore, like a portent. The creative fever—another traditional and fiery metaphor, aligning art and illness, or the abnormal—felt fatalistic. Yet the house fire, which she calls 'a reprimand to the collector', also gave her a vivid sense of escape: 'I felt lucky to wake up, lucky to make the beds, lucky to grind the coffee.' This revaluation of the ordinary and the here-and-now leads her to write about the fire as the kiln in which she reforged her artistic aims. 'I wanted to locate poems in a now that would never recur, in a present [. . .] utterly different from my previous use of that

tense [. . .] I wanted, as well, poems not so much developed as undulant, more fire than marble.'[4] The poem, that is, should achieve the state of the element that enkindled her determination.

In 'Night Song', the speaker addresses a lover asleep on an unidentified shore, beginning 'Look up into the light of the lantern.' This context suggests the myth of Eros and Psyche—the mortal woman enacting the forbidden, gazing at the anonymous god who has regularly visited her bed, and her body, in darkness. In the classical era, of course, that lantern would have held a naked flame: Glück says, implicitly, 'Look into the origins of my own revelation.' The one other mention of fire in the poem is a simile for sexual passion:

> Even our hands are cold, that were like kindling.
> Our clothes are scattered on the sand; strangely enough
> they never turned to ashes.

Here, we hear iambic and trochaic patterns: yet these are often quenched in the poem. Each time it seems that the lines have warmed into a steady metre, Glück's punctuation, semantic emphasis or line breaks stall it, snuff it out. This is appropriately ugly; the half lines blur and bluntly interrupt—thus redefining the title. The poem is no lullaby, nor even a serenade: it is a reveille, a call to consciousness, a song to puncture the night. The speaker wants to awaken the lover, to share more than sexual knowledge:

> [. . .] I know now
> what happens to the dreamers.
> They don't feel it when they change. One day
> they wake, they dress, they are old.

Tonight I'm not afraid
to feel the revolutions. How can you want to sleep
when passion gives you that peace?

The speaker, Glück tells us in her essay, is
on a kind of vigil or fire-watch. She wants to
witness every second of life and growth, every
second of the energy travelling between
herself and her lover. The poem is an
admonishment to behold the present: on the
sleeping lover's face is 'a look of mild expectancy' or passive waiting; its opposite is ardent
action, immediacy. Love lends fearlessness.
Even the alterations, dislocations or agonies
of time are welcomed. (It's very much a young
lover's demand, or at least a demand from a
young phase of love. The poem sequence as a
whole acknowledges this, as it follows the
relationship to a point of separateness, where
the speaker says 'in each of us began / a deep
isolation, though we never spoke of this / of
the absence of regret. / We were artists again,
my husband.')

The burden of 'Night Song' is discordant
with that of the 'Parable of the Burning
House', that ancient verse which tells us that
all our bonds to the earthly present—even to
loved ones—are deluded: cause of all our
agonies. I'm afraid I'm weak. As a reader
seeking solace, I resist the impossible ideals
of the Buddhist text: Glück's poem feels truer
to lived experience. Imminent danger renders
the present infinitely precious. Written in the
light of such danger, 'Night Song' tells us to
relish our present: not to dream, wishing for a
fictitious future. The Lotus Sutra, however,
would say that Glück (and I) are still trapped
within our blazing houses: still clinging to
illusion.

IV

Margaret Atwood's poem 'Morning in the
Burned House' was first collected in her book
of the same title in 1995. Atwood has written
elsewhere on a related motif. Her book
Survival: A Thematic Guide to Canadian Literature
(1972), in a chapter called 'Québec: Burning
Mansions', unpacks the image of the burning
ancestral home, recurrent in French-Canadian
literature, as a symbol of freedom from
stifling, corrupt tradition. Atwood's own
poem, however, is not about the purgative
fires that cleanse us of the disease and sins of
history. Reaching no deeper into history than
the nuclear family, it is an eerily elegiac
meditation on the separations and estrange-
ment that time works between mother, father,
brother, sister.

The poem begins with a prosaic statement
of action and place in the sequel to some
domestic conflagration: a statement which it
instantly retracts. It then carefully compiles an
inventory, tracing a past physical and material
context with simple clarity. And then, with the
kind of God-like ease an author can wield
within a text, Atwood resurrects, destroys and
resurrects this context within adjacent clauses.
It is as if fate is a coin she keeps tossing. The
poem's argument flickers between yes and no,
light and dark, so that, despite its visual acuity,
we're not quite sure what we're seeing. The
work is an almost hallucinatory experience:

In the burned house I am eating breakfast.
You understand: there is no house, there is no
    breakfast,
yet here I am.

The spoon which was melted scrapes against

the bowl which was melted also.
No one else is around.
[. . .]
I can see the swirls of the oilcloth,
I can see the flaws in the glass,
those flares where the sun hits them.

(From lines 1–21)

[. . .] everything

in this house has long been over,
kettle and mirror, spoon and bowl,
including my own body,

including the body I had then,
including the body I have now [. . .]

(From lines 24–29)[5]

The startled repetitions and the strange intensity in those overturned tenses potently re-enact the way the mind revisits trauma. Despite the alertness of Glück's speaker, somehow her poem seems cooler next to Atwood's; it takes me back to the edgy rhythms of life in a decayed, fire-blown building, after the immediate crisis had passed, and the task was to contemplate what changes the experience had wreaked. Atwood's poem, by contrast, is almost pyromaniac: it sets off all the chromatics, all the visual jolts, from the night of the fire itself. The fox-orange flames. Tear-stained faces, dark and pale. The enormous portable footlights the fire crew used to illuminate the charred, dripping interior. Throats of fallen whisky bottles, cocked over the open pit between first and ground floors. Atwood's simple use of colour calls to mind, in particular, the one belonging of ours that was damaged by the fire. It was a wedding-gift from a friend: a print of a work by Edgar Degas, A Maid Combing a Woman's Hair. It is

painted almost entirely in umbers and ambers, as if Degas were trying to show—without depicting the hearth itself—the play of firelight over the women's faces, hair, and clothes. The print is bubbled and stained: not singed, but water-damaged. Torrents from the fire hoses leaked in behind the glass of the frame.

Atwood's poem, like the others, is a meditation upon the force that stains, singes, damages us: reduces us to ash and matter. Although it too is separated by centuries from the Lotus Sutra, it shares Zen-like qualities, seeking to 'boggle the mind and jar it loose from conventional concepts of time and space'.[6] Yet where the Buddhist devotional text uses immense catalogues of myriad beings, and outlines vast stretches of time which ordinary consciousness barely grasps, Atwood tinkers with tinier descriptive cogs. She blurs tenses, uses oxymoron or paradox. The result intercepts with Buddhist notions that 'anywhere is the same as everywhere, and now, then, never and forever are all one'. It is a concept that the Western reader of modernist poetry will instantly associate with the Christianity of T. S. Eliot, whose poem 'Burnt Norton' begins with great, intoning, priestly repetitions and abstractions:

Time present and time past
Are both perhaps present in time future,
And time future contained in time past.
If all time is eternally present
All time is unredeemable.

Atwood's metaphysics are similar—yet the music of her poem is Independent Label to Eliot's Deutsche Grammophon. Sibilance, consonance, assonance and the careful rhyme of metrically parallel, polysyllabic words fuse sound and poetic vision with an astonishingly light hand and enviable insouciance:

[. . .]
as I sit at this morning table, alone and happy,

bare child's feet on the scorched floorboards
(I can almost see)
in my burning clothes, the thin green shorts

and grubby yellow T-shirt
holding my cindery, non-existent,
radiant flesh. Incandescent.

That nexus of sounds says listen closely to the thematic conclusion; it also helps to bind together apparently disparate adjectives. This technique reiterates that there is more harmony between these concepts than might first appear. What glows and is luminous with youth is in the process being consigned and razed. What is burning is already burnt— although the very act of making the poem is evidence that memory reseeds the ash.

V

In Atwood's poem, fire is time. To move from Glück and Atwood to Cilla McQueen is to move from myth and concentrated metaphor to a work more akin to realism. McQueen's 'The Autoclave', published in *Markings* in 2000, is of all the poems discussed here the most direct document of the struggle to accept the material losses (including author's notebooks and drafts) incurred in a major house fire. Aptly, McQueen's metaphor for creativity in this poem is antithetical to flame or fever: writing is taking 'scoops from the inner stream'.

The poem's speaker recollects—one might even say rebuilds—all of the architectural and emotional spaces of her home, The Flounder Inn at Otakou. For me this stimulates a similar imaginative reconnaissance of the rooms and corridors of 'Homelands', our old building at 26 Lordship Park, Stoke Newington. McQueen evocatively remaps the floor plan, and accompanying thought-routines at Otakou. Her spaces return me to the partly roofless and wall-less living room of Flat One. With that return come the sounds of furniture shifting, French conversation, and the mention of a name, all funnelled down through the gaps from the ruined flat above: knocking and echoing like rocks dropped into a cavernous underground stream. Hearing these sounds again reinforces to me that the real shocks of that night were nothing to do with material loss, but rather with what the fire uncovered of people's lives.

Perhaps those watery metaphors above, too, are brought on by McQueen's poem. 'The Autoclave' begins with descriptions of a coastal home, its flora and fauna, the sound of rain. If there is any overtone of threat at all, it might be that the house—the draughty Inn— could flood and float out as jetsam on high tide. The steady rhythms, the stanzas which range from six to ten lines (deviating only as much as wavelets reaching a little nearer, retreating a little farther, along a shoreline), and the continuous present verbs, all lull us into comforting notions of the cyclical, the endlessly renewing. Then—in a mimesis of suspense—a hyphen between stanzas punctures this pattern, tells us to hold our breath, before a deliberately top-heavy two-line stanza dumps us on the shore with its blunt, uncomfortable truth:

> And then the Flounder Inn burns to the ground,
> with everything in it.[7]

In this poem, 'Memory settles / like ash': it signals the backwards glance, a barrier to acceptance. McQueen's account of the 'acute recall' which means that she can 'see and smell and feel / my vanished house' makes 'The Autoclave' seem a sister to Atwood's poem. Yet unlike Atwood, who intentionally retracts tenses to give the reader an uncanny, creeping sense of past and present realities melting into, and ghosting from, one another, McQueen makes it clear that memory is not current reality. She explains, and so undercuts, the illusion, because her purpose is to understand and release herself from the experience: to cremate it, in fact, not to recreate it.

Paradoxically, the crucial manoeuvre for McQueen in this process of acceptance that 'the past is past' is to find a parallel between the house fire and ancestral experience: to achieve a deeper sense of history. McQueen moves into crisp yet detailed, factual narrative, retracing genealogy and a story of origins which incorporates one of the oldest narrative traditions for framing migration: the 'new beginning' in 'fresh pastures'. (And why innovate, when preserving links between the self and historical lineage is the rhetorical aim? We read too narrowly, too superficially, if we reserve critical praise for literary innovation alone.) McQueen's house fire becomes an autoclave—the agent of separation and purification. Just as her immigrant ancestors had to undergo temporary segregation from the wider community, to enter quarantine, so

too the contemporary poet's self has had to undergo separation from some of its false, or 'unhealthy', attachments: to possessions and even the notion that certain hoarded manuscripts and journals could be the source of future work.

So the house fire becomes a threshold, allows passage into another world: entry into a new home, a new relationship, and new bonds with this partner's whanau. The final stanza of McQueen's long, meditative work frames memory as both self-absorption and itself an essential autoclave. Recollection is a process of isolation within, and eventual purification from, loss: necessary before the community can be rejoined and the self can look outwards again, becoming receptive as well as reflective.

> Memory's mirror backing peels,
> partly opaque and part transparent,
> lacy, disintegrating
> until the reflection disappears entirely
> and the world shows through.

VI

What all the works here share—Eastern gathas, American essay, American, Canadian and New Zealand poems—is the transmutation of a specific (even if fabulous) event, into an archetypal contemplation of the nature of time. Rereading them all does open up answers to my enquiry about why I've been unable to address the London house fire in poetry—or more specifically, in the lyric poem.

Initially, sitting in the repaired living room of 'Homelands'—screwed up notebook pages littered around me like useless paper-starter for a campfire when there was neither coal nor wood—I thought that I might have hit a failure of descriptive language. The house fire wasn't 'like' anything I had ever experienced; therefore the metaphors and similes I tried were inadequate, false. Yet having eaves-dropped on the structures built by other writers, I now think the problem lay else-where, in my choice of the lyric form itself. The lyric poem homes in on the essential, the prototypical. It finds the still points in the turning world. Usually, that is, it doesn't tell a story.

In the already bizarre, twilight zone usually reserved for deep sleep, the fire brought together—or into collision—a chaos of people and attitudes. The house fire affected ten people, of five nationalities and diverse historical and political backgrounds, in the building. And it affected others in neighbour-ing houses, whose homes were also endan-gered. To write authentically about that night would require a dense map of an even denser social matrix. I would need to write about the experience of immigrants and expatriates in London, social masks, alcoholism, a severe self-neglect, apathy and squalor, suicidal and even murderous impulses. I'd have to write about cross-cultural love affairs, homosexual-ity, prejudice, fundamentalist religion, sexism, language barriers, prostitution, and a degree of mental illness of which, at that time, I had virtually no practical understanding. And I would need to write about the destruction of my own then-still-young assumptions. One of which was, if you smile kindly, and ask someone how they are, and offer friendship, and they smile back, saying they are fine—

then either all is fine, or you have at least helped to make things a little finer than they were. In other words, I had to learn that decent human kindness cannot always heal.

On the night of the house fire, watching giant tentacles of flame probe through shared ceilings and floors, I'd felt shrunk and rattled, reduced to dice in the hands of the cold. On subsequent days, the flat was freezing: the fire had sucked all heat from the surrounding space, yet my cheeks were constantly hot: coals of memory and shock.

Fire hoses had turned the soot into an ankle-deep, wet, black sludge in the main hallway. Three of the flats were badly dam-aged, and the whole building was clogged with the sickly, sweetish stink of carbonised wood, rice, plaster, coffee, wallpaper, leather, wire, fruit, carpet, vinyl, foolscap, plastic, milk, wool, linoleum, cotton, bread, Formica, paint, nylon, cardboard . . . Once so innocu-ous in its solidity, the entire physical world now seemed like tinder. Every substance concealed its true volatility. For several nights—irrationally—I slept in my clothes, expecting to be woken again by the clatter of crisis. Time and again I replayed in my mind's eye the desperate image of the tenant who had started the house fire and failed to call the emergency services. Face begrimed and tear-streaked, eye-whites red with smoke, hands held out as blackened claws, this person had surfaced, hunched, from the building, with a police officer at each arm, and dressed—surreally, it seemed at the time—all in green, like wood that wouldn't take.

Thinking about this emergence and what linked us all to it, and thinking too about the structures and salvations of poetry, I realise the fire was in many senses a single loop in a complex net. For the written word to act effectively as spill or touchpaper for a fuller illumination, it would have to convey those complexities. I suspect that if I am ever capable of writing about that house fire in a wider sense than I've managed here, it would be in some narrative—not lyric—form. For, as the scorchingly articulate Glück has said in another article: 'only narrative can adequately represent in art the onset of harm.'[8]

Notes

1. Glück, 'The Fear of Happiness' (the Hopwood Lecture), PN Review 118, Nov–Dec 1997, p. 56.
2. Watson (trans.), The Lotus Sutra, New York: Columbia University Press, 1993, p. 69.
3. Glück, The Triumph of Achilles, 1985. This and all subsequent quotations from the poem come from Glück, The First Five Books of Poems, Manchester: Carcanet, 1997.
4. Glück, 'The Dreamer and the Watcher', Proofs and Theories: Essays on Poetry, New Jersey: The Ecco Press, 1994, pp. 99–100.
5. This and all subsequent quotations from the poem come from Atwood, Morning in the Burned House, London: Virago, 1995.
6. Watson, translator's introduction to The Lotus Sutra, p. xv.
7. This, and all subsequent quotations from the poem, come from McQueen, Markings, Dunedin: University of Otago Press, 2000.
8. Glück, 'Story Tellers', PN Review 117, Sept–Oct 1997, p. 13.

My thanks to Andrew Johnston and Christine Lorre for past introductions to certain poems and poets.

Riddles (i)

1
my bone
takes my flesh
to your lips

2
my wings
sweep earth
from the earth

3
you walk
on my head—
my neck, your ankle

4
my jaws
hold down
the roof

5
dreaming
I cover you
like cloud

6
I burn,
illuminate your
feast of me

Riddles (ii)

'No part of the gannet was ever wasted.'

Make a spoon of my breastbone
and of my wings a feather broom.

My head makes a soft shoe laced at the throat,
my beak a stout peg, to anchor the thatch.

Featherdown is your bed in the storm.
I give strength to your body

and brightness to your eyes—
your lamp is my clear oil flame.

The Landfall Review

ARCHITECTURE

Prying Eyes:
The Greer–Frith House
By Douglas Lloyd-Jenkins

In 1959 John Greer and Richard Frith decided to build a house in Ranui, a suburb in west Auckland that even now many contemporary gay men, fortified by thirty years of political activism, would think twice about before making their home. Challenging though the location of Greer and Frith's new house may have been, what made their decision unceasingly provocative was that they commissioned a house made of glass.

Rectangular in plan, the Greer–Frith house is essentially a flat-roofed glass pavilion. The exterior walls of the house are large sliding panes of glass separating roof and floor (although the short wall of the house, separating the bedrooms from the carport, is sheathed in vertical wooden battens). The floor and roof go beyond the exterior walls to provide a covered deck around three sides of the house and a carport on the fourth. The house is an essay in the simplicity and clarity of modernist structure, made possible by the combination of then-innovative steel framework and ordinary timber construction.

Inside, services, such as the bathroom and laundry, are arranged within a central core that is lit and ventilated from above by a lantern roof. One side of this plywood-clad core features an entrance while a kitchen and dining room area are located on the opposite side. Adjacent to the solid wall of the carport

are two bedrooms. The opposite end of the house is dominated by a large living space that can, when necessary, be divided from the rest of the space by sliding shoji screens.

The house does not announce its presence to the casual passer-by. It peeks momentarily from behind roadside plantings. The front door is positioned discreetly at the side of the house. Approaching the Greer–Frith, one senses the ease with which the house nestles on its site. Once inside, it becomes apparent that those first impressions are the result of a seamlessness of conception and execution which characterises every aspect of this elegant house. The visitor seems to glide through the barely delineated rooms, through a structure delicately poised between interior and exterior space as traditionally understood. The floor flows away, while, above you, the roof does the same. Both planes carry the eye off into distant space—over dramatic views of Auckland harbour. It's a home that seems to transport you, in a perfect equilibrium, through its interior and back once again to its front door.

Greer, whose business was women's shoes (Frith was a violinist), furnished these spaces in an elegant and urbane variant of modernist taste that seemed to defy the house's semi-rural setting. The architect made sure that interior materials lacked pretension, choosing simple pine-veneered plywoods, cork flooring and white acoustic ceiling tiles. To this the men added locally designed furniture that, like the house itself, nodded knowingly to the aesthetics of Japan and Scandinavia. New Zealand art, including works by Binney, Brickell, Ellis and Illingworth, hung throughout the house, but in a manner that drew

The Greer-Frith House, Ranui, Auckland. Architect: Tony Mullan. Photographed in 1992 by Bill McKay.

attention to the shared philosophies of artist, architect and client rather than to the status of the client as collector. When photographed for Home & Building in 1960 the house was as complete a vision of assertive modernism as any yet built in New Zealand. However, the significance of the house lies only partly in the decor choices of client and architect.

Whether John Greer and Richard Frith would consider themselves queer or even gay is a moot point. Like American architect Philip Johnson—who also dwelled in a glass house—or Australian novelist Patrick White, homosexual men of the same generation, they were not necessarily comfortable with the developments of a post-liberation gay culture. Yet when two homosexual men chose to live together in a glass house in full view of the prying eyes of a homophobic land, they were perhaps knowingly, perhaps unknowingly, pioneering a more inclusive New Zealand architecture, and opening the way into its more pluralistic spaces. No matter how they themselves may have seen it, Greer, Frith and their architect Tony Mullan prised open a queer space in the monotonous expanse of post-war New Zealand building.

Tony Mullan is an architect whose star has faded somewhat since his death in 1988. Born in 1922, he trained at the Auckland School of Architecture and in 1949 established Rigby.Mullan in partnership with fellow student Alan Rigby. They quickly established a reputation as designers of smart modern houses. By 1960 they were entering a highly productive decade in which they designed two spectacularly successful Auckland commercial buildings—246 Queen Street (1965) and the White Heron Hotel (1967)—both now

effectively destroyed by ham-fisted alterations.

The key to understanding Tony Mullan's diminished reputation is the fact that neither he nor Alan Rigby taught at the Auckland School of Architecture in later life. This career choice almost guaranteed that they and their work would be excluded from the canon of modern New Zealand architecture. It also severely limited their impact on subsequent generations of architects. The loss was a major one, because the provocation offered by the Greer–Frith house was not only social, it was architectural. In retrospect it seems precisely what New Zealand architecture of the '60s and '70s needed.

For the larger part of the twentieth century, the New Zealand house, whether designed by architect, builder or owner, has seldom been a place that celebrates living. Instead the service offered by architects was largely one of concealment. Architects hid the individuality of their clients from prying eyes. The result is a darkness, both literal and spiritual, at the heart of the New Zealand house. Together with an indisputable solidity, this darkness is probably the defining characteristic of much of our domestic architecture. It was, after all, a domestic architecture, conceived almost wholly in the service of the family unit. Consequently the New Zealand house is dominated by a prosaic desire for welfare and security.

Solidity is the primary measure of good architecture in the pragmatic land of the pioneer. Even after the mid-1930s, when modernism offered greater freedom of form and expression, the New Zealand house remained indisputably solid. The architects of the '40s and '50s—whether it be

Christchurch's stately moderns, Wellington's embattled émigrés, or Auckland's celebrated Architectural Group—were seldom able to transcend the notion of architecture as an act of physical enclosure. Consequently there is something relentlessly tenebrous about New Zealand houses before the Greer–Frith.

One imagines that, in the late '50s, those couples confident enough to approach an architect at all were more often than not served up pre-existing solutions based on family units and suburban conformity. John Greer and Richard Frith were freed from those limitations by their homosexuality—in a period when homosexuality offered few obvious freedoms. Tony Mullan understood the possibilities that such freedom offered an architect and local architecture. To walk through the Greer–Frith is to witness that understanding in action, Mullan reorganising the priorities of architectural space so as to reflect the way Greer and Frith lived. The result is a house in which welfare and security are sidelined or at least refashioned. In the Greer–Frith house, solidity is replaced by grace, and light penetrates darkness at every point. It is a structure less concerned with housing (shelter from future dangers) than with living (pleasures taken in the present tense). The daring suggestion of Mullan's house is that life could indeed be good.

With the Greer–Frith, Mullan prefigured the planning and structure of many subsequent New Zealand homes. This is not to say that the New Zealand houses of the '60s and '70s were glass boxes, or indeed even open spaces. Quite the opposite. For the next two decades architecturally designed houses tended to turn increasingly inward, offering combinations of small womb-like rooms held together by complex multilevel planning. Mullan suggested, however, that a house could represent more than a life of conformity. He suggested that, even in a Protestant land, play was neither wrong nor unserious, that lives could be lived individually, and that beauty could be contemporary. Forty years later, these ideas undergird contemporary New Zealand architecture. It is an achievement for which Tony Mullan, the pioneer, has received little credit.

As for Greer and Frith, the choice to live one's life in full view seems, retrospectively, avowedly contemporary and consciously queer. Although they were pioneer inhabitants of this new light-filled and pleasure-giving space, Greer and Frith well understood the pragmatic land in which they lived. In the same way that the two men knew that floodlighting the surrounding trees at night kept moths at bay, they also knew that this puritan place was inhabited by prying eyes that needed to be artfully distracted. To ensure that their lives as gay men could function fully, they, again like their contemporary Philip Johnson, built on the same property a near-windowless cabin. This bunkhouse retreat served as the site of indisputably queer activity. Here, as inhabitants of public and private spaces of their own creation, they waited for the land around them to change.

On the Waterfront

By David Mitchell

The American architect Mario Madayag didn't take long to find out that Aucklanders were either dismissive of their city centre or blind to it.

'When I first got here I said to my New Zealand friends, "Let's go to the city." "What for?" they wanted to know. I began to wonder if there was any appreciation of architecture here. Everywhere in the world people take you to their city. In New York and Paris they talk about architecture. But here they're too busy fishing.'

Mario is one of the designers of a master plan for four blocks of downtown Auckland. With Auckland architects Jasmax and American landscape architects Peter Walker and Partners, he won a big competition for the Auckland City Council's waterfront design. The proposal reworks lower Queen Street and all the land covered by the old Post Office, present bus terminal and parking building, plus many heritage buildings between Customs Street East and Quay Street, owned by the City Council.

A few years ago there was an infamous Britomart Scheme for this area—private office towers were to be built over an underground bus terminal. The mayor and city council were widely condemned for supporting it, and when the scheme failed after a staunch campaign of opposition, a new council launched an 'ideas competition' for the area.

More than a hundred serious entries were submitted. Public comment on the proposals was invited, and, as Mario could have pre-dicted, respondents showed a strong preference for any development that included water, grass and trees. Politicians had called for a 'gateway to Auckland', now promoted as 'First City of the Pacific' (a reference to time rather than prowess, I take it).

People looking for a gateway might be disappointed in the winner. They may see palms on Quay Street, but no equivalent to the Sydney Opera House is likely to lure them into Auckland. Madayag, Jasmax and Walker have so far produced only an urban framework with landscaping, but they foresee a development that is a bit like The Rocks in Sydney. Decency prevails. Financially, politically and architecturally, the master plan offers the minimum of risk, and that gives it a reasonable chance of being realised.

The designers make an extremely optimistic case for a relatively low-rise 'urban transport village', ringed by existing heritage buildings. It is to be a 'pedestrian-friendly' neighbourhood revitalised with 'diverse land uses', including 'alternative urban living and working environments'.

Underground tracks will bring suburban rail into town, linking the present railway station to a new terminus in the old Post Office. The old bus terminal building is to be replaced by a ring of bus stops around one or several of the blocks closest to Queen Street. I doubt if either of these manoeuvres will do much to clear Auckland's choked transport systems. Relatively few people travel by train now, and those who take buses may find no more comfort on a winter night at a row of bus stops than in the present draughty terminal. Facing continuous bus stops has never appealed to ground-floor tenants either.

The designers have reclaimed as an extension of Queen Street the unpopular QE2 Square in front of the Post Office. Like several other entrants in the competition they have run Queen Street through to Quay Street, and extended it into a Queen's Wharf Park. That is common sense, and it will improve the downtown development that was the city's last urban design disaster.

Less understandable is the decision to put a new square—the 'Ta Huhu Market Plaza'—behind the Post Office, enclosed by substantial buildings to the north and west. In the cautiously upbeat jargon of such proposals, the designers see it as 'a marae—a place for celebrations, parades, performances and protests'. A celebration behind the Post Office? I'd rather go fishing.

Mario Madayag quickly detected the public wariness of architecture here. Unlike many of the also-rans, the winners show pictures of landscaping but none of new buildings, which appear merely as diagrammatic blocks, similar in scale (pretty low) to the heritage buildings that surround them. The winning scheme preserves old patterns of settlement, and extends pedestrian and vehicular transport linkages into the surrounding city and out to the wharves. The proposal pre-empts criticism by avoiding what is most likely to cause offence. It avoids architecture.

Why the fear? A lot of Aucklanders have

'Three-dimensional soundbites': underground station with basalt volcano cones. Image courtesy Jasmax Architects.

been offended by nearby commercial developments. On the site of the old railway yards there is a new and tawdry commercial strip that might have been lifted from the outskirts of Las Vegas, and an office park that could have come from the industrial fringe. There have been strong objections to the new 32-level AMP tower being built along Quay Street, and there is now a justified mistrust of developers, and a palpable antipathy to office blocks.

Yet there is nothing intrinsically wrong with high-rise buildings. They form the great twentieth century vernacular from which Manhattan, Hong Kong and Rio de Janeiro are made. There, density counts. Even in downtown Auckland, I wonder if the transport village of the Madayag–Jasmax proposal will attract a large enough population to sustain itself. Since it is so well-connected, couldn't the site be developed at higher density without overwhelming the historic buildings which encircle most of it? It is a measure of the oddness of this city's architectural make-up that the only agency capable of saving historic buildings, and *averse* to building its own money-making high-rises, is the city council.

Despite my doubts about it, I have come to accept the Madayag–Jasmax scheme for its lack of pretension. This is no easy admission, coming from a fellow-competitor whose group proposed a glass bus terminal and a couple of high-rise towers to play off against the heritage buildings. Seven- or eight-storey blocks have worked fine around the world. In essence this is what Mario and his colleagues propose for Auckland.

Still, the project represents a triumph of mildness over vision, and this lack of vision is

nowhere more apparent than in the lumbering metaphors of the 'local' with which the design has been embellished. Compared with the fundamentals of an urban design, the decoration or enrichment of the architecture with art might seem trivial. But it is those aspects which newspaper reporters typically seized on in their search for a local stamp in the scheme.

Mario consulted two artists, Richard Thompson and Michael Parekowhai, and proposed various sites for collaboration with artists. He sought spatial and colour conceptions in local art, including the paintings of Colin McCahon, and he tried to lock European urbanism into Maori interpretations. When I heard him referring to McCahon as a source in his proposals I wondered if he was not ticking off cultural references as diligently as he ticked off planning ones. Others will wonder how anyone can call a street full of buses and cabs and light rail an 'urban marae', while maintaining a straight face. Can a 'kauri forest retail courtyard' a floor below street level on the most uninhabitable part of the old QE2 Square really refer to 'Mana Whenua Tane Mahuta (forest)' and 'Papatuanuku (the integrity of the land)'?

This is not architectural thought. It is marketer's persiflage, a froth of weightless metaphors. Down in the underground station there is to be a row of basalt 'volcano cones' between the tracks, each with a 'volcano oculus' admitting light from above. It seems to me these emblems of the landscape above are important neither as art or architecture, but as a form of three-dimensional soundbite.

Geoff Park wrote in the last *Landfall* of our increasingly touristic view of nature: 'Like our plundered coasts, the forests need their people back. Not visitors treating them as scenery, but people who consider them home . . .' Park's concern for wild nature is similar to mine for the city, an ecology no less deserving of care and passionate habitation. In proposing obvious local themes in urban landscaping (like the present tui-tiled seats of Queen Street), and making prefab emblems of local natural features, we sell New Zealand-the-Beautiful to ourselves. We become tourists in our own city.

With that cautionary thought in mind, Aucklanders can at least be grateful that the council abandoned the bad old Britomart scheme, and has lined up a new and civilised alternative. All they need now is the comprehensive transport strategy which should have preceded the whole exercise.

Neurotic White Mice
By Tessa Laird

At Home in New Zealand: History, Houses, People, edited by Barbara Brookes (Bridget Williams Books, 2000) 256 pp., $49.95

At Home in New Zealand grew out of the University of Otago sponsored symposium 'The Idea of Home in New Zealand' which took place in November 1998. In fourteen chapters At Home traverses a significant amount of territory: from the Gothic Revival in Victorian architecture, to New Zealand authors' relationships to puritanical ideas of home and family; from the first Labour government's state housing schemes, to the controversy over the 1964 School Publications Branch booklet Washday at the Pa.

Each essay is thoroughly researched, liberally footnoted, and some even boast flow charts to better illustrate the changes in the shape and scale of New Zealand housing throughout the country's history. 'The Justification for Labour's Housing Scheme: The Discourse of "the Slum"', by Penny Isaac and Erik Olssen, is a veritable orgy of statistics, and while I'm sure that the percentage of houses lacking a water-closet pan in the Dunedin Housing Survey of 1938 is of prime importance to experts in the field, it's hardly compulsive reading for the curious browser.

At Home is plainly not for the coffee table. There are moments of rich, heartfelt, evocative writing, but those moments are deeply embedded in starchy academic discourse. Still, there's enough variety in At Home to find at least one thing you like. Fancy some background on early welfare homes? Ever wondered about the demise of domestic service? Then this is the book for you.

My personal highlight was Anna K. C. Petersen's 'The European Use of Maori Art in New Zealand Homes', with photos of the remarkable Rehatui, J. H. Menzies's house in Banks Peninsula. Petersen recalls the fashion of Pakeha christening their homes with Maori names, real or fabricated, 'supposed to designate the carefree life of the "pre-civilized"'. I believe the South Seas answer to Sans Souci, the unforgettably awful Waiwurri, still stands on Franklin Road in Ponsonby, Auckland.

Although two of the chapters deal with Maori issues, it's clear that no chapter is written from a Maori perspective. Since the original symposium was titled 'The Idea of

Home in New Zealand', it's surprising that no one chose to examine the notion of the ancestral home, the marae, and its changing face over the centuries. Instead, *At Home* traces the trajectory from colonial house to state house, deviating only slightly to record a little modernist architecture for good measure.

Indeed, in 'Book, House, Home', Justine Clark and Paul Walker point out that modernist architects assumed that an 'indigenous' architecture would be based on early settler buildings rather than Maori models. And while it might seem anomalous that such recent imports to New Zealand soil could pass for indigenous, Ian Lochhead points out that when Roger Walker took his reinterpretation of the colonial house to the Homeworld Housing exhibition in England in 1981, 'forms that 130 years earlier had served to remind British emigrants to New Zealand of their homeland now looked alien on British soil'.

Robin Skinner's 'Home Away: A State House in London' details an earlier example of New Zealand exporting its architecture to the motherland, this time a state house at the 1950 Ideal Home Exhibition. It's surprising how long the list of 'distinctly New Zealand' features is: four-by-two timber construction (in native woods), terrazzo bench, kitchen joinery, the copper, electric hot-water cylinder, concrete wash tub, trellis fence and clothes line.

I asked my grandfather if it was this display, or something similar, that had inspired him to move his family from Chessington, Surrey, to Panmure, Auckland, in the early '50s. He said that he hadn't seen the show home, and that there was just as much 'awfully crummy' housing in New

Zealand as there had been in England. It was the thought of 'warm weather and plenty to eat' that attracted war-weary Britons like him to a better life in the colonies. Even Skinner admits that it was the ample supplies of meat, honey and butter on display in the Ideal Home kitchen, more than the quality of the joinery, that likely impressed British visitors to the exhibition. In 1950, the British were still suffering food rationing.

Talk about 'assisted emigration': it cost my grandfather all of two pounds and sixteen shillings to shift his family across the world, so eager was New Zealand at the time to fill up the population gaps opened by war casualties. While listening to my grandfather reminiscences, I realised what was missing from *At Home in New Zealand*. Although it's subtitled 'History, Houses, People', very few personal stories, or portraits of individuals, are allowed to emerge. Instead, general statistical patterns are preferred, which prohibits engagement with the texts on the intimate level that the domestic subject seems to warrant. The only chapter in which an individual character does emerge strongly is 'Sarah Campion and the Modern Colonial House' by Xanthe Howes and Paul Walker. Sarah Campion wrote for *Home and Building* in the '50s, and is cosmopolitan, witty and insightful. In a vivid writing style, she describes her longing for a home that 'does not look like an igloo, a discarded corset box, a kitchen tidy, or a sanatorium for neurotic white mice'.

The only other personal stories in *At Home* are the biographical snippets of writers' lives we get from Lawrence Jones's 'A Home in This World? Provincial Writers and the Puritan Family'. Jones reminds us of the bad old days of repressive sexuality, homophobia, overzealous temperance and Sabbatarianism. Typically, writers eschewed accepted notions of 'home' and preferred to live in shacks and derelict rented rooms. While Jones talks of Robin Hyde, Frank Sargeson and Janet Frame, two other chapters begin (and, a little too neatly, end) with Katherine Mansfield references. That both Charlotte Macdonald and Helen M. Leach use Mansfield as a springboard is a fair indication of the historical bias of At Home—the essays move slowly from the 1850s to the 1960s, but the last thirty years remain uncharted. Not only that, but the South-Centralism (and I'm talking Clutha, not Compton) is a little over-whelming, with none of the contributors hailing from Auckland and very little of the discussion focusing on what is obviously the largest conglomeration of houses in the country.

Mansfield's double cameo reinforces the assembled writers' predilection for literature over other art forms as a reflection of the home in New Zealand. Visual artists are mentioned only twice: Macdonald refers to Frances Hodgkins's watercolours of a servant girl, and Jones quotes the autobiography of Toss Woollaston. Brookes does say in her introduction that this volume is intended only as a blueprint, 'patchy in some areas . . . and likely to be redrawn many times'. I have visions of future volumes featuring cover art by Ava Seymour, from her controversial *Health, Happiness and Housing* series of photomontaged human anomalies outside state houses. Not to mention the early works of Merylyn Tweedie, who cut up and recombined '50s advertising for household appliances to comment on gender issues (some ads of this kind are reproduced in *At Home*).

To labour the architectural metaphor: *At Home in New Zealand* feels like a good solid foundation, and an awful lot of detailing, but now it's time for some furnishings, frivolous decoration, and, well, *living!*

From the Ground Up
By Damian Skinner

Looking for the Local: Architecture and the New Zealand Modern, Justine Clark and Paul Walker (Victoria University Press, 2000) 206 pp., $59.95

This book cracks open a remarkable time capsule. At the heart of *Looking for the Local* lies an unfinished book project started in 1957 by the Architectural Centre, a Wellington organisation of architects and other interested parties who sought to stimulate debate about architecture and 'good design' in New Zealand. An attempt to survey post-war architecture in this country, the book was left uncompleted—a victim of competing agendas about what it should be and of economic imperatives (the book failed to find an international co-publisher). In what amounts to a story of treasure in the attic, its presence unsuspected for years, Justine Clark and Paul Walker found the box of photographs and assorted material in the Alexander Turnbull Library. As they write in their introduction, *Looking for the Local* 'is based in that box: it revisits those debates and the material collected so as to re-examine the architecture of mid-century New Zealand.'

The Architectural Centre's book was never completed because there was no agreement about what kind of point it should make about New Zealand architecture. Should it be a polemic, focusing on the house, a highly mythologised site of New Zealand identity in architecture? Should it be a more general survey, in which New Zealand identity emerges more gently from the variety of buildings featured? National identity is the key to understanding the book's failure, and, in the authors' eyes, it becomes key to understanding the nature of modernism, and the interaction of the local and international in New Zealand, during the '40s and '50s. As the authors note, 'For architecture, the desire for the local was intimately bound up with the commitment to being modern', and thus: 'The conjunction of the local and modern, then, is a fundamental issue in New Zealand architecture.'

Looking For the Local is a kind of postmortem exercise, a book about a book that was never published, and about the material—photographic and textual—that Clark and Walker can exhume for evidence of the kind of life it lived before being interred in the Turnbull. This focus can be construed as limiting, especially in a photographic sense, since many of the illustrations in the book are little more than grainy, taken-on-the-fly snapshots, never intended for publication. Criticism of the authors' effort, where it has been offered, has fixed on the obvious limitations of such scholarly exhumation. Clark and Walker, the argument goes, have wasted their time on some peripheral issues of modernist architecture in this country—

treating a box of fragments as if it were the ark of modernism—rather than writing a much-needed survey of post-war architecture.

How successful the authors have been depends on what you think are the central issues for understanding architecture during this time. Clark and Walker use the book's failure as a usefully conflicted starting point, believing, I think, correctly, that the insurmountable disagreements articulate some essential truths about New Zealand architecture and the wider culture of that period. And their attention is always drawn by what's not represented in the box, or the ways in which the material can suggest the wider context it belongs to. That there was going to be a book leads them towards a discussion of what architectural publishing was like locally and internationally during the period in question. The special attention given to the house as a possible direction for the book becomes an opportunity to explore the mythologised status of domestic architecture in debates about New Zealand architecture generally and the issue of New Zealand identity specifically. Autopsy always gives way to the imperatives of archaeology.

In many ways I like Clark and Walker's attention to this specific pile of photographs and papers, since it represents something of the actual way in which history comes to us: raggedly, in pieces, and at odd angles. Where so much critical discourse in New Zealand is woefully inattentive to the subtleties of historical periods, Looking for the Local proves its worth by taking the tensions and complexities of the moment it surveys as its fundamental starting point. Sure, this book is not a survey of post-war architecture, but I for one

Matamata Grandstand, Architect: Jones, Adams, Kingston and Reynolds.
Photographer: Barry McKay.

appreciate the authors' refusal of a coherent and authoritative account of New Zealand architecture in favour of one that is necessarily more arbitrary, but a great deal more interesting and useful in capturing the all-but-forgotten tone and tenor of debates of the period. Far from being evidence of a fear of taking on a big historical survey, the fragmentary and incomplete nature of the material, and the readiness of Clark and Walker to let this affect their narrative, reveals a willingness to build history from the ground up, detail by fugitive detail.

Moreover, it's a discussion that reverberates beyond the world of architecture. Whatever impact the book has on local architectural discourse, its discussion of the tangled and fascinating relation between the local and the international also offers fresh ways of looking at wider visual culture in New Zealand, from design to painting and sculpture. Clark and Walker argue that in the '40s modernist architecture in Europe became concerned with local characteristics, rejecting the ungrounded placelessness and wilful internationalism of preceding phases of modernism. So those New Zealand architects who went looking for the local were never, as has been insinuated in the past, practising a closed-minded nationalism in defiance of the international. 'By taking the local seriously, New Zealand architects could in turn participate in an international community on terms other than the pre-war ones of Empire.' On the compelling evidence of *Looking For the Local*, writers on the visual arts of this country might profitably spend more of their time looking for the local too.

POETRY

Antipodean Hipster

By Ian Wedde

The right foot of the giant, Mark Young (Bumper Books, 1999) 76 pp., $19.95

Beware the onset of old-fartness in the reconstitution of cultural canons. Much as I enjoyed and celebrated the appearance of the *Big Smoke* anthology of New Zealand poems 1960–1975, it was not without a tremor or two of guilt, fear and shame that I recognised also its air of momentousness and was reminded of my own pretensions at the time. While avoiding the canonical earnestness of academic salvage (or, thank god, revision), wearing its excellent scholarship lightly, and for the most part avoiding the hagiographic, the book nonetheless (and unavoidably) reconstituted as cultural mass a disparate body of writing and activity that was often unaware of its own synergies at the time it was happening.

It was great to hear Mark Young reminiscing on the radio programmes that Chris Bourke put together to mark the publication of *Big Smoke*. He sounded just the same as I remembered from Auckland in the '60s. I was aware, though, that thirty-something years had passed, that during all of them Mark had been silent (to us) and living in Sydney—just as, during his time in the '60s Auckland scene that revolved around the Kiwi Hotel, Barry Lett Galleries and the Wynyard Tavern, he had been distant from and pretty much unheard by the rest of New Zealand.

Most of the poetry activity that was going on in New Zealand during what will probably come to be known as 'the *Big Smoke* years' was not that interested in the rest of the country. It was certainly not much interested in 'New Zealand literature'. There was no big statement involved in this—again, nothing hegemonic—it was not particularly anti-nationalist or cosmopolitan, though there were and are cosmopolitans among 'us'. Largely through the combined agencies of music and politics, there was a surge of feeling connected to a global culture—not of being 'influenced' by, but of being part of, an international culture. It was happening on the cusp of modernism, and was as much about escaping modernism's obscure sense of cultural quality control and anxiety as it was about engaging with political freedom movements and popular culture.

Memory without the assistance of any record more reliable than nostalgia is not going to produce a reliable account of what happened. At its worst, nostalgia will produce 'memoir', the kind of account that always trumps the play with a first person pronoun. Here's mine—for what it's worth, the best way I can find of connecting Mark Young's voice on the radio last year with the 'internationalism' of 'the *Big Smoke* years', and the marvellous coincidence (not) of his poems finally getting published by Bumper Books—*The right foot of the giant*.

My memories of Mark in Auckland are of poetry readings at Barry Lett Galleries and at the Wynyard Tavern. Dave Mitchell was part of a double act that combined the rhapsodic, the laconic and the hip. Wreathed in clouds of cigarette smoke, through which I still see art works by Ralph Hotere and Colin McCahon, as though smoky nicotine were one of the cultural pigmentations of the '60s; with lots of flagon red wine from the Henderson valley, drugs that were subculture rather than mainstream entertainment, and the jazz of Thelonious Monk ('Round Midnight'), these occasions set my youthful benchmarks and probably gave me much of the life I've had. For which I am most grateful.

To be cool was the thing. Looking now at the books of poems I obsessively and anxiously hoarded during the '60s and '70s, I find Grove Press's 'Evergreen Book' series, many of City Lights Books 'Pocket Poets Series', Totem Press in Association with Corinth Press. There are books in here that got buried later in the '70s; they are LeRoi Jones, *The Dead Lecturer*, 1964 (whose cover photo of LeRoi is uncannily like the cover photo of Mark on *The right foot of the giant*), LeRoi's *Preface to a twenty volume suicide note*, 1961, Frank O'Hara's *Lunch Poems* of 1964 (in which, in *Personal Poem*, he has lunch with LeRoi). In the shelf with them, also dusty, the first anguished, homoerotic novels of James Baldwin. One of my sons has my old heavy vinyl Bluenote recordings of Miles Davis, Hank Mobley and Thelonious.

In the same space of bookshelf archaeology, Editions Gallimard *Poésies complètes* of Jules Laforgue ('Je m'ennuie, natal! Je m'ennuie, / Sans cause bien appréciable . . .'), and other *fin-de-siècle* French business, soon converged upon by the bracing intellectual *ennui* of mid-century existential *flâneurs*.

The atmosphere in Barry Lett's at a '60s poetry reading was full of male strut and posturing, but also of a kind of homoerotic anxiety and grief. There was a cultural axis in the evenings which was knowing about the white hipster connection between Black American rhythms, the liberated subject (Frank O'Hara's 'I was walking along the street . . .'), and the suicidal, sophisticated ennui of French existentialism ('L'enfer, c'est les autres'—Jean-Paul Sartre in *Huis Clos*, epigraph to Mark's poem 'No exit'). Sounds weird now, but then it was as global as hip-hop is now.

And Mark Young was the moment's guru in New Zealand. *In memoriam: Robert Desnos* (1969) genuflects towards the French poet; in sharing a conversation about a woman the poet(s) may (or may not) have made love to, the poem has that tone of homoerotic conspiracy over the female sexual object that characterised much male writing then; the rhythms are the syncopated ones that black American poets found in bebop jazz; the poem's subject is the fully disclosed, confessional, intimate first person of the poet himself.

Described like this, it sounds awful. It wasn't—I guess it isn't. In the case of 'wasn't', and my own unstable memoir, the poem is still astonishingly of its time and place. I have no idea how it might read to someone who wasn't there, who isn't (now) in their mid fifties, and I'm not going to try and guess.

```
Black
       gamin
                  disdains all games
     of chance

                      (from 'Gonna roll the bones')
```

In these lines I can still hear LeRoi Jones's poem 'For Crow Jane (Mama Death'. As I heard it then. The elegant, intense swivel of rhythm, whose purpose is to be a precise choreographer of emotion, as well as to be funky. And there are the other rhythms, in the language, its neat riffs and chords of assonance, the casual virtuosity, the throwaway sense of coolness as a style.

This was such a distinct moment, and so short-lived—it was not the Beats of the '50s (though they are in there, they have become kind of naive), and it was not yet what came along soon in the lyrics and music of Jim Morrison, and international solidarity against the war in Vietnam.

Nor am I talking about the jocular, music-hall poetry of the English 'Merseyside' poets, who were as unlike the white hipster thing as you could get—who wrote 'Your finger, sadly, has a familiar ring about it'. Even though Mark wrote his own, almost counter-version, of the Adrian Henri roll-call of cultural icons, it's interesting, now, to spot the differences—in Mark's list are Tristan Tzara, Burroughs, Akira Kurosawa, 'Charlie Mingus & LeRoi Jones', Miles Davis, 'Rimbaud Verlaine & Baudelaire', Jean Genet, Anaïs Nin, 'Basho Cocteau Jean-Paul Belmondo', 'Diana Ross & The Supremes', Frank O'Hara, Pierre Reverdy, Paul Eluard, Otis Redding, 'Ray Charles & Terry Southern', and so on—not a sign anywhere of the Anglo-Saxon heritage, nor, in any shape or form, of its colonial entrepot. Of the Beatles, only hipster Lennon gets the nod from Mark; the others might as well have been pantomime clowns.

Reading *The right foot of the giant* is terrific, but it's also terribly sad, because (on the memoir level) it reminds me of a cultural moment that was intense, brief, poised between a neurotic modernism about to implode and an onrush of popular culture into the mainstream, astonishingly specific in its international signifiers, precocious and posturing but also very cool, and now gone forever.

But not quite—because the people at Bumper Books, in their great wisdom, have rescued Mark's part in the 'moment' for those of us who were sent unsteadily on our life's path by it; and for those for whom this book should be a surprise and a revelation.

Stoned on a Beach
By Jonathan Bywater

Laminations, Murray Edmond (Auckland University Press, 2000) 56 pp., $19.95

Laminations bears witness to an experience of life in Aotearoa that has found sustenance in a sometimes embattled allegiance to often imported 'high culture'—to European literature, modern painting, the university . . . Alert to the dictions of the arts faculty and current affairs journalism, the book addresses the uncertain plight of such allegiances in an age of the 'knowledge economy'.

The poem 'Ballad of the Book' is perhaps the ballad of *this* book. It describes an adolescent identification with exotic modernism by some 'Young male arrivistes / with open mouths'. The author's note glosses the poem thus: 'Michel Seuphor's book *Abstract Painting* . . . and Ahmad Jamal on piano at The Persching, NYC, 16 January, 1958 meant life was looking up in the '60s in Hamilton.' From

God's eye view, Picasso's paintings and Jamal's tinkle through 'Surrey with a Fringe on Top' were hardly at the forefront of innovation in their respective media by the '60s, but Edmond's poem shows how they might have been differently received in a particular place. A sense of world-expanding hope is won from the radically new experiences they represent to the characters in the poem. This promise resonates with the scattering of references to the author's continued affection for 'difficult' works. Through the rest of the book his touchstones include (as will be no surprise to readers familiar with his work) Dada, surrealism, situationism, John Cage and Amiri Baraka. A conviction in the value of this cultural legacy is clear.

Later, Edmond somewhat awkwardly lampoons a local philistine voice:

> . . . Beware
> 9. of wankers, turds in teacups, smartarse *girls*
> 10. who want to make the culture *interesting*.
> 11. We don't need that here . . .

The sentiment 'we don't need that here' could well come from the Waikato of the early '60s, but, in this poem, 'Counsellor to Client', we hear it in the context of contemporary consultancy and counselling. Edmond suggests a new variation on high culture's unpopularity. Here, more than just making you a wanker, it may be economically foolhardy. Edmond's response to these specific contemporary politics is something I'll return to. He also responds to a broader indictment of avant-garde traditions. Their revolutionary ambitions have, of course, been long contested, and, internationally, the political

promise they once may have offered is no longer widely credible. Edmond himself has been scolded for his supposedly pretentious and dated allegiance to 'making it new' (witness Jane Stafford's review of *The Switch* in *New Zealand Books*, reprinted in *Under Review* in 1997). So how does he accommodate his (post)modern(ist) inheritance?

The local relevance of this stuff is at issue. Edmond's poetry answers by vigorously evoking the local and its connections to the rest of the world: the Holocaust, foreign writers and the business of travel are woven into the poems in an Auckland-centric way. The key strategy, however, conscious or not, seems to be to keep things light. The success of this poetry is the way its authorial voice can drop in such a rich range of allusions and quotations. Things we may not have heard of are gently skipped over, or touched on and let drop. Robert Desnos and his ilk are kept safely at quotation's length. The poetic effects here are not out to raise themselves to the purple heights of surrealist invention.

The strongly aural quality and pun-heavy playfulness of Edmond's last two books, *Names Manes* (1996) and *The Switch* (1994), is retained in *Laminations*, but absorbed into a conversational voice which inherits a lot from what John Newton has called the 'personable' qualities of Edmond's '70s writing. The pithiest formulation is Michael Harlow's: 'composed talk'. So, for example, while Edmond uses words that declare their use in theories—'dialectical reality', 'presence', 'desire', 'signifiers'—he does so not with the theoretically loaded self-consciousness of a L=A=N=G=U=A=G=E poet, but in a way that honestly records everyday undergraduate parlance, the mundane verbal bric-a-brac of academic life. Eschewing the neatly plain and lyrical, Edmond wants these high cultural linguistic artefacts accepted as part of the scenery. Likewise he deploys *Listener* column business jargon and political buzzwords ('outsourcer', 'marketeer', 'upskill'), and even high poeticisms that others might strive to avoid ('gimlet', for example, 'limned', and two uses of 'murmurous').

His alert ear achieves some pleasing renditions of colloquial phrases: 'put it in the too-hard / basket', for instance, or 'How do you mean?' The syntax is spoken. Lines approach us without haste, with friendly asides, soliloquies or letter-like chat, several of these poems bearing dedications and addressed as if in the second person. The rhythms and cadences that sound through the variously shaped stanzas are almost always conversational, regardless of his curiously diffuse and varied use of open forms.

There are relishable moments of delicacy:

To walk is to remember; your feet are thematic.
('Starfish Streets')

My body is lighter than freckles

('XSFXU2')

Enjambment and line breaks are rarely crucial to the sense, and often seem quite arbitrary. Alongside this looseness, though, the historical avant-garde does inform the book, again with a certain lightness. The use of language is self-conscious. The likes of Shakespeare, Aristotle and Heraclitus wave out from behind phrases. Here and there Edmond drops a coin in a mental juke box, and phrases come out to a popular tune:

All those years ago (ago!)
('Two Wing Circus')

the music goes round and round . . .
('No Skiting Here')

The sounds of words select some titles ('Can That Mango' (can that man go) and 'XSFXU2' (excess affects you too)), while others *look* right ('No Skiting Here' (no skating here)), and some pun simply ('Small Fry' (small children and small fish) or 'Curiosity of the First Water' (literal littoral water too)). The title of the book itself is a typical word play. That laminations is a typo or homophonic slip away from lamentations is spelled out by the first of the clutch of epigraphs, from the biblical Lamentations. The similarity of sound suggests in joking fashion that these 'sore wailings' (as I will soon describe, there *is* something of a rueful tone to the poems here) have been fixed under a glossy coating for display. Any attempt I make to take the allusion further, though—away from weak pun towards 'resonance', perhaps—seems to slip through my fingers: Edmond as Jeremiah? Well, no. Auckland as Jerusalem? Huh? (Baxter, Ringatu?!) The play is frustrating in an uninteresting way, as the sense is too clearly resolved. The pun is awkward and lopsided, closer to a deliberate malapropism.

Treated with this lightness, the ideas that attach to the words and allusions can seem glossed over. In the first two poems Edmond finds room for play in the rickety everyday terms describing the political spectrum, and he gives them a quick shake:

Now the left has been made right & right made left
('Rant for Mickey Joe')

The middle of the road is now the centre
('Two Wing Circus')

An importance is suggested by the repetition, but the way these lines relate to the rest of the poems leaves them vague and undeveloped. The relative subtlety of the latter play is promising, but the poem fails to engage its possibilities. The lack of stability discovered in the terms, the sense of confusion the writer can evoke with them—a deconstructive ploy, if you like—is not used to open up new possibilities but rather to stimulate a mood of nostalgia and regret.

The poem 'Escapade from Culture into Archive' is likewise limited by this regretful tone. The poem is a mishmash of buzzwords and puns that effectively conveys a mood of despairing puzzlement. To say 'No two pianos add up / to the same cultural dollar' sounds rueful, and knowing. It is another coded token for those of us who understand the joke in 'Some of our best reviewers / have never read a word.' Or know the Creative New Zealand world mockingly invoked in 'let down let down / your yellow application.' But where does this leave us?

The poems fail to do more than to evoke a sense of disempowerment, as if we (the 'you' often implied) will nod and smile. The author declares his commitment to certain cultural values and enterprises, but misses the resources they offer him. Although the book in 'Ballad of the Book' is 'held tight', it is 'hardly read, only looked at, touched'. Apart from the limitations of the craft and formal appeal, it is ultimately this lack of engagement with the language used—its sources and potential uses in thinking the present mo-

ment—that limits my appreciation of Edmond's book. Name-checking revolutionary thinkers and writers, working to acknowledge their place in our landscape, is one thing. Working with them, demonstrating their usefulness, is quite another. If Jane Campion in 'Escapade . . .' is 'still a prisoner / there in the myth / of the lonely land', then this poet himself is sounding a bit lonely. In the end he leaves us 'Stoned on a beach / with Darien', where 'Whatever uh-huh / serves your yeah.' We're left, that is, feeling a connection with someone at least, but still on the outside, knowing bad politics are going on, feeling apart from it, and ultimately at a loss.

Yin, Yang and Young
By Iain Sharp

The Spit Children, Jo Randerson (Victoria University Press, 2000) 104 pp., $19.95

From the Author of, Nick Ascroft (Victoria University Press, 2000) 72 pp., $19.95

The connective tissue here is obvious—two gifted young New Zealanders present their first collections in the same year from the same publisher. But because they've pursued different paths to VUP's door, it's tempting to play up the contrast and depict Randerson and Ascroft as opposites, representatives of rival modes, yin and yang.

Randerson takes the well-travelled route to publication—via the creative writing course at

Victoria University, supervised by Bill Manhire for the last quarter of a century. Like other recent VUP productions from Manhire alumni (Jenny Bornholdt's *These Days*, Virginia Were's *Jump Start*, Duncan Sarkies's *Stray Thoughts and Nosebleeds*), *The Spit Children* is a miscellany, comprising six poems and thirty-seven prose pieces. The latter resist easy classification, occupying ill-defined territory between the short story, the dramatic monologue, the prose poem, the stand-up comedy routine. Indeed, given Randerson's proclivity for splitting her work into small units, some with titles of their own, even my arithmetic might be challenged. Depending on the way you count, the tally could go as high as fifty-three prose splinters. I think 'you said' is verse and 'Jesus was a very nice guy' is prose, but a reverse decision would not be unrespectable.

Confusing? Yes, but I doubt if local readers will be fazed by the book. VUP miscellanies have become a recognisable part of our culture. Manhire has generously revealed the working methods of his course in interviews and in the anthologies *Mutes and Earthquakes* and *Spectacular Babies*. We know that course members are urged to try their hands at different genres, thereby generating miscellaneous portfolios. And the assignments that Manhire favours often call for an atomised (or itemised) approach. 'Write a short story (or poem) which consists of three false starts. Your text should be composed of three numbered fragments (1, 2, 3), yet still—somehow!—complete. Give the overall piece a title.' Randerson satirises these exercises in 'Mary and the King': 'Think up four clever and appropriate titles for this piece. Choose from the following . . .' This kind of mickey-taking

is hardly unusual among Manhireans. A bit of cheek at the instructor's expense is par for the course.

As the back cover of *The Spit Children* readily divulges, Randerson was one of Manhire's star students—winner of the prize for best portfolio in 1996. But her whole curriculum vitae brims with achievement. Head girl at Wellington Girls College in the early '90s, she scooped the Bruce Mason Playwriting Award in 1997 and is the 2001 Burns Fellow at Otago University.

Ascroft is more of a maverick. But that's not to say he's without antecedent or analogue. Host of the Fuel Café poetry readings in Dunedin, he has clear links with the crowd-wowing troubadour tradition, back to Baxter and the *Big Smoke* generation, via David Eggleton. A high-speed word-juggler, heavy on assonance, onomatopoeia and internal rhyme ('The wangles one wangles / To flaff out of the spout of some bungled manhandled clutches'), Ascroft seems indefatigably image-conscious—'the author of', primarily, himself.

Beneath magnificent tresses, he surveys us from the back cover of his book with an enigmatic smirk. He looks like a rock star—the young Robert Plant, say, or Robin Williamson from Incredible String Band, or Dee Snider from Twisted Sister. And in several poems he strikes a pose beloved by rock luminaries for the last four decades: the visionary debauchee who persists in his Dionysian ways in spite of impending doom and the tut-tutting of squares and wowsers. One offering ('Corpse Seeks Similar') is narrated from an Accident and Emergency ward, another from a rescue helicopter. 'Let's drink ourselves daft, you & me,' he recommends in 'Three Provincial Cuckoos'. Dunedin is derided for its 'Presbyterian starkness' ('the plain browns and crucifixion reds'). 'I'll laugh a prayer to the bar,' he promises in 'Red Letter Daze'.

The most startling piece of image-mongering, though, is the book's front cover. It reproduces, about half-size, one of the curiously named Art Wolfe's superb colour photographs from *Primates* (Chronicle Books, 1997). Almost any of Wolfe's animal portraits would make a striking cover. Ascroft could have chosen the cherry-crowned mangabey, the snub-nosed langur, the red uakari, the douroucouli. But he opts for the aye-aye—a rare arboreal primate, found only in the coastal forests of northern Madagascar. A harmless creature, agreeable even (its name a double affirmative), the aye-aye has been persecuted for centuries because of its demonic appearance (glowing nocturnal eyes, foxy face, bat-like ears, weirdly elongated fingers). Many Malagasy villagers kill it on sight. A misunderstood monster—is that how Ascroft sees himself? Or how he imagines others might see him?

Although fond of allusions to the animal kingdom, Ascroft does not furnish us with a dissertation on the aye-aye. Unfairly picked on, threatened with extinction, this small grub-eating beast would be more at home in Randerson's book, I believe, than in Ascroft's. This is the point where the cartoon-like oppositions I've been building—head girl versus headbanger, prize-laden protégée versus prolix profligate—start to crumble. Both writers are more various, slippery, and surprising than the caricatures I've suggested.

That's what makes them interesting.

For such a conspicuous winner, Randerson shows a strikingly Sargesonian tendency in her fiction to side with losers—low-status workers in dead-end jobs, ridiculed freaks and eccentrics, the abandoned and those who fear abandonment, wheelchair boys, people with broken-down washing machines. She has a flair (strengthened by years of hard work in the theatre) for mimicking the vague, hesitant speech patterns of the semi-articulate and not overly bright. 'I don't, I couldn't . . . I didn't know what was going on,' says Sarah in 'The Tale of Sarah and Himintheyami'. Many of Randerson's characters might say likewise.

The fairy tale told in dumb-cluck modern vernacular is one of her favourite strategies. ('There was this bear, right, this angry, angry bear, well not so much angry, this weary bear, he was very tired and stuff . . .') But she apes the dolt-on-the-street's reductive view of other kinds of venerable lore too. Her blending of Friedmanite economics with the loaves and fishes parable from John 6:26 is particularly funny: 'It's very important to look after those people who are getting all the fish. Otherwise it will never dribble down.' Her condensed version of *An Angel at My Table* is equally deft: 'Frame, a lady writer, had trouble with menstruation. Left a stain on the chair at school. Felt very embarrassed. Slid out of class.' And she closes the book with a sly rewrite of the Easter story that transforms the Messiah into a Houdini act: 'Jesus was a very nice guy and when he died they used a big rock to stop him getting away . . . The rock that they used was big. Jesus got out anyway.'

Beneath the deadpan drollery, though, a moral earnestness and an exceptionally bleak world view distinguish Randerson from other Manhirean ironists. Cruelty, belligerence and betrayal are the norm in her imaginative terrain. Rape, mutilation and murder aren't that uncommon either. In the story that gives the collection its title, two men quarrel and one punches the other in the head and spits on his offspring. 'You are the children who grow from the spit,' says Randerson, but to whom is she talking? The children of the '70s? Or all of us, irrespective of vintage? I take the salivary baptism to be universal, not tribal. And what, in Randerson's estimate, does life hold for us after this insalubrious start? More gobbing, further punches. That's about as hopeful as she gets. My response to *The Spit Children* is like my attitude to Woody Allen movies. I skip the pessimism, since I have plenty of my own already, and head straight for the jokes.

Ascroft is cheerier—not exactly sunny-natured or encouraging, but flourishing at least a genial brand of nihilism. Despite the rebellious air, he's more interested in reverie than revolution. Characteristically, the title of his opening sally, 'Deserter Slips Away', is a multi-layered pun. Set in a sandy dream landscape, complete with camels and cacti, the poem gestures towards the Saharan 'emptiness of our marrow'. But, yes, Ascroft's bardic stance is definitely more day-dreamer and deserter than ranter, reformer or revenger. And that includes absconding from his own elaborate metaphorical constructions. No sooner has he built an ingenious Ludwig II castle-in-the-air than he wants to shift to a new address.

Take 'The Diagnosis or Parable of Jupiter's Eye', for instance. In 1601, Galileo named the moons of Jupiter after the boss Olympian's

extramarital flings: Io, Europa, Callisto and the dazzling Trojan youth Ganymede. Ascroft pictures the giant planet as a 'great red eye' and Ganymede, its largest satellite, as 'a conspicuous mote'. A poet with a philosophical cast of mind, steeped in the classics—Fleur Adcock, say—might weave this suggestive material into a wry meditation on how the beloved becomes first blind spot then blight. But that's too tidy for Ascroft, too closed and conclusive. His poem is presented as a dialogue between 'the doctor' (an Adcock-like metaphysician) and an 'I' who grows impatient with the reasoning, feels 'forced to cut in', and takes the discussion in fresh directions with the tale of a telescope-wielding relative whose eyes 'ghosted over'.

The pleasure in reading Ascroft is in watching this quick-witted improviser conjure forth metaphors, mythologies, word-music, then deconstruct them in a flash. Just as the portrayal of Randerson as exemplary Manhire graduate, while partly true, tells only half the story, neglecting the gloomy-pants outlook and bolshie politics, the lampooning of Ascroft as neo-hippie egotist misses the twinkle in titles like 'Horse-Frightener Pins on a Spray' and 'Hobbledehoyed Senescence Ahoy'. He doesn't just strike poses, he knocks them to pieces. He's out the door and off home, whistling, while the rest of the room are still trying to figure out what he meant by his entrance.

ART

Bearing Witness

By Laurence Simmons

Parihaka: The Art of Passive Resistance, edited by
Te Miringa Hohaia, Gregory O'Brien and Lara Strongman
(Wellington City Gallery, 2000) 232 pp., $69.95

> Those who are bent by the wind
> Shall rise again when the wind softens
> — Tohu Kakahi

I

Every ten or so years on the gallery circuit
there is an exhibition which reassigns curatorial boundaries and defines the future of
expositional, even critical, practice. These
exhibitions have not necessarily contained the
best or most representative examples of
current New Zealand art, nor have they been
the most popular with artists or the viewing
public. One such example was Francis
Pound's 1983 Auckland City Art Gallery
exhibition entitled *New Image* which framed
New Zealand images in the context of the
recent styles of contemporary American art.
The painters selected for his exhibition, Pound
declared, 'paint new images for New Zealand,
and paint them in a new kind of way.' There
was also the novelty of seeing our images in an
international context, since for these painters,
Pound went on to argue, 'a New Zealand
identity in art is, now, a dead question.' The
subsequent protracted debate on the national-
ism/internationalism of New Zealand art
practice during the '80s could not have
occurred without the stimulus of Pound's *New*

Image exploration. Similarly, the multifariously
curated 1992 exhibition entitled *Headlands*
inaugurated the 'fun-park aesthetic' of the
new museology which has sadly dominated
not only curation but also museum construction here in the '90s. *Headlands*' cheap shots at
one of its more senior participating artists in
catalogue essays, its corny juxtaposition of
painting and popular culture, and its shoddy
social historicising caused another participating artist Richard Killeen to re-baptise it
'Hatelands'. Despite (or was it because of?)
this bad faith, *Headlands*' populism can be said
to have initiated a (still ongoing) decade of the
'Te Papa-isation' of New Zealand art.

I believe that *Parihaka: The Art of Passive
Resistance* is just such another 'redefining'
exhibition, one which provides a pathway for
future curatorial practice. It is deliberately a
visual mishmash: historical photographs and
contemporary ones (in particular a stunning
sequence by Laurence Aberhart), personal
sketches, eyewitness accounts and drawings,
poetry (by J. C. Sturm, Alistair Te Ariki
Campbell, Dinah Hawken, Robert Sullivan,
Cilla McQueen, Ian Wedde, Chris Orsman,
Elizabeth Smither, Roma Potiki and Apirana
Taylor), careful historical study and recon-
struction (by Hazel Riseborough following on
from Dick Scott's pioneering work *The
Parihaka Story* and then *Ask that Mountain*),
commissioned and even recommissioned
artwork (by Colin McCahon, Ralph Hotere,
Tony Fomison, Michael Smither, Nigel Brown,
Barry Brickell, Don Driver, John Hovell,
Stanley Palmer, Para Matchitt, Laurence
Aberhart, Anne Noble, Michael Shepherd,
Darcy Nicholas, Séraphine Pick, Pauline
Thompson, John Walsh, Chris Heaphy, John

Pule, Shane Cotton, Brett Graham, Fred Graham, John Baxter, Tame Iti and Natalie Robertson), contemporary song (Brian Potiki and Tim Finn). The complex protocols and processes to put together such a heterogeneous mix were negotiated by Wellington City Gallery staff over a period of seven years and involved, for gallery staff, a new way of working with a community entailing the building of trust as well as the sharing of power and decision-making.

Walking around this exhibition, or perhaps one should more appositely say 'ploughing through' its divers layers (in the Wellington City Gallery the exhibition was divided into four large sections), and negotiating the interplay of the historical, the institutional and the personal, the literary and the visual, is a complex and layered experience which triggers multiple forms of memory both collective and individual. While I was in the gallery a group of visitors, breaking into squeals of delighted recognition, came upon photographs of themselves as children in a glass case. I was reminded of two European traditions of image collection. One was the Jewish *yizker-bikher*—historical commonplace books of communities produced collectively and made up of statistics, historical narrative, biographies of leading citizens, interspersed with eyewitness accounts, personal sketches and reflections, summaries of folklore, even drawings, maps and photographs. Most *yizker* books were compiled in response to the Holocaust and are the equivalent in words and pictures to communal tombstones memorialising a life that has vanished. The Jewish-Maori connection is suggestively explored by Professor Paul Morris in his

catalogue essay and I want to return to it in a moment. I was also reminded of the walls of certain Catholic churches where one finds a corner, often the niche of a favoured saint, crowded with notes to the Virgin Mary, hopeful plaques, painted images and beaten-silver body-part relics, inscriptions of all shapes and sizes, words snatched from a private but also a communal tragedy. For in all these instances we find survivors speaking for the dead through forms of collective memory.

II

Parihaka is paradoxically one of the most shameful episodes and one of the most gripping stories in New Zealand's colonial history. Under the compelling leadership of two *rangatira*, Te Whiti o Rongomai and Tohu Kakahi, the settlement of Parihaka on the slopes of Taranaki became a refuge for thousands of Maori dispossessed and made homeless by land confiscations. Government land confiscations were then to include the Parihaka block itself. To test the legitimacy of Government land seizure Te Whiti and Tohu employed a strategy of removing survey pegs, ploughing, planting and erecting fences on surveyed land. On 5 November 1881 the village of Parihaka was invaded by a militia of 1500 settlers under the command of John Bryce, the then Native Minister. Offering no resistance, hundreds of the followers of the community's spiritual leaders Te Whiti and Tohu were arrested and suffered transportation and imprisonment for years in the South Island, where many died from harsh prison conditions. Over several months in a war of attrition the prosperous and self-sufficient village of

Parihaka was systematically razed, homes were looted and burnt, crops destroyed and livestock slaughtered. Maps were finally redrawn in an attempt to obliterate the memory of Parihaka from the face of the earth.

In September 2000, almost one hundred and twenty years later, Associate Minister of Maori Affairs Tariana Turia was to use the term 'holocaust' along with the notion of 'postcolonial traumatic stress disorder' to describe the impact of the Crown's actions at Parihaka and the subsequent effects of colonisation upon the people of Taranaki. Turia's speech inflamed much media controversy and self-righteous indignation concerning the 'improper' use she had made of the word holocaust, eventually causing the Prime Minister to issue an edict banning all use of the term on the part of her ministers. However, it should be pointed out that the 'correct' use of the term holocaust is itself 'incorrect' and the history of an incorrect term may also prove instructive. 'Holocaust' is the scholarly transcription of the Latin *holocaustum* which, in turn, is a translation of the Greek term *holocaustos* which means 'completely burned'. The semantic history of the term is thus essentially Christian, and paradoxically it was used by the Church Fathers both as a polemical weapon against the Jews, to condemn Old Testament sacrifice, and also as a laudatory term, to glorify the sufferings of the Christian martyrs. Even Christ's sacrifice on the cross is ultimately defined as a holocaust by St. Augustine.[1] So, given this history of semantic migration, the real question around the use of the term 'holocaust' in a New Zealand context concerns the notion of collective memory and its function.

We need to be reminded again here of the distinction to be made between public history and collective memory. I am referring to the rupture noted by several commentators between modern historiography, its fact-gathering and technicity, and the ritualised forms of meaning-bestowal of collective memory shaped by folklore, the Bible, literature and art that transmit and recreate the past in an organic fashion in a self-reparative process of handing down wisdom from generation to generation.[2] This is the real issue in the holocaust analogy, the issue of history in relation to memory, the issue of what refuses to disappear. Here again we must not underestimate the crucial importance of images and symbols in keeping events 'before our eyes' and the responsibility so engendered towards the represented subject. In the imperative to make everything visible the viewer's eyes are fully implicated, and we are made aware of our silent and detached glance as spectators removed in time and place.

At the same time, as they begin to circulate among a wider populace, we need to be attentive to the sanitising of the images of Parihaka where its potent symbols may easily become trite (I sense this has already happened with the *raukura* image of Michael Smither's *Ask that Mountain* (1973) used on the cover of Dick Scott's book). Such instances are further proof that the issue of how memory and history become art is always a complicated one. The exhibition catalogue testifies that what consistently exercised Government concerns at the time were the political not the spiritual dimensions of Parihaka. This point is voiced strongly in an essay by Ruakere Hond:

Gordon Walters, *Te Whiti*, 1964, alkyd enamel on hardboard, private collection, Wellington. Photograph courtesy City Gallery, Wellington.

Images of passive resistance are prominent in references to Parihaka, where the plough has become a symbol of peaceful protest as much as it is a tool of cultivation, where associations are made with Gandhi to demonstrate the success of this strategy of resistance, and where the Bible is portrayed as a source of inspiration for this initiative. If Parihaka is limited to such a narrow focus of representation we are all the poorer . . . The true value of Parihaka is in its historic ability to innovate the assertion of Maori authority.

The many works on paper of Ralph Hotere in this exhibition, his 'ploughings', explore the notion of sovereignty and land rights together with the metaphor of textual inscription into the land. Hotere does this through a combination of formal drawn lines which suggest the inscribing of lines into the darkness of the earth through the process of ploughing and by the literal presence of texts—proverbs and *waiata* and their translations, poems by Hone Tuwhare and James K. Baxter—dug into the fabric of his paintings, which allow the political message of Te Whiti and others to go on reverberating. Exhibition co-curator Gregory O'Brien in his insightful essay notes how Hotere's works 'assert the

Gordon Walters, *Tohu*, 1973, PVA and acrylic on canvas, private collection, Auckland. Photograph courtesy City Gallery Wellington.

human presence in the natural environment' since 'the ploughed line in the landscape has an analogue in the line left by the tattooist's chisel or needle. Traditional Maori moko is a furrow drawn into the human skin.'

Michael Shepherd's *Negative* (2000) is a meticulous transcription of the details of an 1881 photograph of Parihaka from the Alexander Turnbull Library. But here Shepherd's earthy-brown worked impasto gives a materiality to the ploughed ground which the black and white photographic original could not capture. The tiny painted fracture lines of the shattering of the glass negative (transgressive plough lines in their own right) are an intimation of the political reverberation of the events at Parihaka. Shepherd's only addition to the bare facts of the composition is a white flag, or more precisely a white ground ambiguously inscribed 'their flag' where a flag ought to be. In this crucial play of signs it is important to remember, too, that the only artworks in this exhibition to engage with the legacy of Parihaka which were generated entirely from within an artist's oeuvre—that is, were not commissioned and solicited by a curator (either James Mack in 1972, or the organisers of the 1981 Parihaka Exhibition & Art Auction held at the Govett-Brewster Gallery, or the curators of the present exhibition)—are *Te Whiti* (1964) and *Tohu* (1973) by abstract artist Gordon Walters. These two black-and-white examples of Walters' *koru* series, painted ten years apart and of almost equal dimensions, stand like sentinels to one of the main sections of the City Gallery exhibition. In his ambitious large work, *Stereo (Tohu and Te Whiti)* (2000), the younger artist Chris Heaphy attempts to engage in a dialogue between Tohu and Te Whiti but also one between Walters and himself. It is anomalous, I feel, that in the accompanying catalogue McCahon's *Parihaka Triptych* (1972) is accorded the status of two fine catalogue essays (by Wystan Curnow and Jonathan Mané-Wheoki) while Walters merely receives a one-page statement (illuminating as it is) from his widow. There has been as yet no real widespread understanding of the ethical and political dimensions of Walters's particular combination of Maori cultural influence and Western modernism.

III

We continue to face with greater sensitivity, but also with an increased sense of impotence and weightlessness, murderous racial politics: genocidal episodes in Cambodia, 'ethnic cleansing' in Rwanda and Bosnia . . . While there are clear distinctions to be made between a 'Final Solution' aimed at the extermination of every Jew and the obliteration of a village, its inhabitants and their vision, these events do raise the same questions about our species. Are we, can we consider ourselves, truly human—part of a 'family of man'? What about the veneer of progress, culture and educability we claim to embrace, and which in this case Pakeha colonialism purported to bring its subjects? So it is that the focusing power of the story of Te Whiti and Tohu which links us to their past also links them to our future.

These fundamental moral questions are not over, as Tariana Turia tried to argue; they are not simply part of a history (and thus forgetfulness). Anyone who comes into contact with them is still gripped, finds detachment difficult. How *not* to talk about them is the challenge. This is the 'stress' of the postcolonial for both sides. How do we approach such a dark moment of our past? What does forgiveness or reconciliation mean? Especially in circumstances when the offence may not be forgotten. The issue of response cannot be separated from that of responsibility. How do we handle, as both Pakeha and Maori, the imputation of collective guilt? In 1999 in a public lecture entitled 'Forgiving the Unforgivable' in the Auckland Town Hall, the French philosopher Jacques Derrida explored the Latin origin of 'pardon', its meanings and usages in French, English, and German, and the way they carry over *aporias* of 'the gift', 'giving', 'forgiving', 'forgiveness' (*donner, le don, pardon*). With great seriousness and understanding he played off their ambiguities, exploring their multiple meanings in various texts, and their valencies in contemporary contexts: the Holocaust, decolonisation, ethnic conflict, crimes against humanity. And, as he concluded, 'forgiveness is an impossible truth or an impossible gift.'

Art as a performative medium, not art reduced to official meaning or information, has a chance to transmit this 'impossible gift' as a counter-force to manufactured memory since, despite its imaginative licence, art is more effective in embodying historically specific ideas than the history-writing on which it may depend and draw. Indeed, one thing that does counteract the despair and enforced silence around the Parihaka story is the surprising energy and creativity that has eventually emerged from the initial devastation, the artworks that have been returned as literal gifts to the people of Parihaka. The artists, photographers and poets gathered in this exhibition and its accompanying volume of essays and images have erected signposts which allow future cartographers to chart a new ethical territory in which we can orient ourselves. We are only at the beginning of an understanding of this 'politics of memory' and Parihaka: The Art of Passive Resistance shines like a beacon at the beginning of the twenty-first century to guide us towards a new shape of knowing.

Notes

1. See Giorgio Agamben, Remnants of Auschwitz: The Witness and the Archive, translated by Daniel Heller-Roazen, New York: Zone Books, 1999, pp. 28–31.
2. See, for example, Maurice Halbwachs, La mémoire collective, Paris: Presses Universitaires de France, 1968, and Yosef Hayim Yerushalmi, Zakhor: Jewish History and Jewish Memory, Seattle: University of Washington Press, 1982.

Fear of Flying
By Lita Barrie

Rather than capturing the spirit and energy of art from the Pacific Rim, Flight Patterns—the big show that finished in February at the Los Angeles Museum of Contemporary Art—became a show less of art than of social studies. Most of the art looked like dusted-off '70s educational bulletin boards on the evils of environmental degradation and colonial imperialism. Despite the curatorial invocation of the radical politics of turning attention towards the Pacific Rim (as opposed to Europe) the exhibition had the jaded feel of a parade of old-fashioned lefties proud of their struggle as artists on the periphery—or as peripheral artists, which here amounted to the same thing.

This emphasis upon pedantic social commentary—rather than the poetics of place—merely served to marginalise art from the geographic margins. This kind of social commentary is a sentimental and self-indulgent form of the death of art, relying upon the institutional framework of a museum for its audience of the converted while at the same time shrugging off the need for visual innovation or complexity. It cannot compete with mainstream documentary as an agent for change in the real world.

The unrelenting dreariness of room after room of environmental protest images, blasted social landscapes and banal urban architecture made viewing this exhibition feel like a duty—but to no purpose. Clearly, the work on show here has less to do with the shared topographical approaches to landscape alluded to in the title—with the sense that there might be patterns connecting our various flights and migrations—than a curatorial fascination with the politics of oppression. The danger is that the artists are chosen to illustrate a perspective that is preconceived, and thus patronising, rather than arrived at through close engagement with the art itself. This kind of token representation gives the impression of a vanity show. Would an exhibition from a major European art centre showcase this kind of self-pitying subject matter? Would their governments help fund the export of art that wallowed in its own cultural oppression?

The declared purpose of the exhibition was to loosely connect work from the Pacific Basin with work from the American West Coast through the broad metaphor of 'flight patterns'—which was stretched to mean anything from topographical views, in-flight mappings in aeroplanes, migrations, immigrations, transience or displacement. From this touristic perspective, the exhibition linked photography, film, video and painting by contemporary Canadian, Australian and New Zealand artists to early and contemporary Southern Californian artists. Of the twenty-two artists (and one artists' group) included, most were drawn from Southern California, confirming that familiar preferences lurked behind the exhibition's putative embrace of 'other' Pacific cultures.

The exhibition's flight around the Pacific 'took off' with early works, from 1955 to 1958, by Californian photographer Paul Outerbridge. Taken for travel articles he wrote for magazines, these luscious colour photographs of the California–Mexico border show the topographical impulses of early American photography at work in a new urban landscape. The flight then fast-forwarded to Antony Hernandez's black-and-white images from the late '70s and early '80s of banal sites of leisure and transience around Los Angeles.

Here the exhibition flew forward again to a group of contemporary California photographers—Allan Sekula, Christina Fernandez, Miles Coolidge, and the collaborative Center for Land Use Interpretation (CLUI)—who explore photography's historical relationship to the social landscape. Still drawing upon the tradition of topographical photography that originated with the recording of late-nineteenth-century Western expansion, these artists examine the urban and ex-urban terrain in pictorial series using more conceptual strategies. Thus Sekula used still photography and slide projections to explore the late-capitalist transformation of maritime economies in his documentation of the protests around the recent World Trade Organization conference in Seattle. Fernandez juxtaposed images of sweatshops around downtown and eastern Los Angeles with texts about the fear of deportation. Coolidge explored the death of architecture in blank images of ship containers converted into migrant labourers' housing. The Center for Land Use Interpretation explored an overlooked part of the California desert in a gesture that proved ineffective as activism while really stretching the workable application of the word 'art'.

Having established Californian photographic and conceptual strategies as the point of departure and return for a flying tour of art by artists from more remote areas of the

Pacific Rim, the exhibition took in a disproportionate number of hand-wringing white males who appropriate bicultural symbolism to protest the wrongdoings of their own race and kind. This kind of ingratiating tactic ensures said artists a place in *every* artistic power play—demonstrating how easily defiant gestures can be both domesticated and exported when they are really transparent ploys for approval. Having seen Tim Johnson's artful appropriation of Aboriginal dream paintings accommodated comfortably by a variety of curatorial rhetorics in New Zealand and Australia, and having seen his work a week before in New Zealand, I cringed to see him again in Los Angeles. The inclusion of the ubiquitous Tracey Moffatt to represent the angry Aboriginal female voice was equally predictable.

Also predictably, the New Zealand component of this Pacific fly-by focused on the displacement of Maori culture from perspectives of white guilt and Maori indignation—represented by Laurence Aberhart and Michael Parekowhai, respectively. While Aberhart's haunting documentation of vestiges of New Zealand's past delves into many layers of cultural complexity, the selection of his most well-known photographs for this exhibition was disappointing and an obvious indication of a superficial take on a body of work that is worthy of more in-depth exposure. The half-sceptical, half-reverential allusion to Colin McCahon in Parekowhai's man-sized word sculpture *The Indefinite Article* was lost on an LA public which was unfamiliar with McCahon's work and which, moreover, could not be expected to relate to an island mentality that mythologises one artist alone. Gavin

Hipkins's photographic series *The Unhomely* lost less in transition, through cleverly ironic Freudian motifs which offered multiple points of entry into a complex treatment of the New Zealand landscape and the myths that code it.

Flight Patterns was a novelty exhibition for MOCA which established Los Angeles's claim to have created the 'pattern' for imitations of its own topographic and conceptual strategies all over the Pacific Rim. The organisers went looking for their own reflection rather than discovering something new—which is a pity because they overlooked some work that could have intrigued an LA audience. Having made a tourist swoop over the Pacific Rim, MOCA has fulfilled its quota of art from the peripheries and will now in all likelihood return its attention to the art centres—American and European—which for better or worse remain the model and measure for such institutions.

The exportation of New Zealand art into this patronising perspective on the Pacific was a pyrrhic victory for the New Zealand participants. The artists were chosen to represent their culture rather than themselves, functioning as mascots instead of having an artistic voice of their own. It is revealing to compare such exposure with the world attention given to New Zealand film-makers like Jane Campion, whose work has entered the culture on its own merits. *Flight Patterns* was a sad demonstration of the difference between artists who have what it takes to represent themselves and those who cannot (or choose not to) fly on their own.

CRITICISM

Talking About Stead
By Karl Miller

The Writer at Work, C. K. Stead (University of Otago Press, 2000) 288 pp., $39.95

I think I should declare an interest, and a lack of interest. I read Karl Stead's book on modernism, The New Poetic, when it first came out, and have long admired his writings, some of which I published in London journals. I am also a seasoned admirer of the poems of his mentor, confederate and friend, across the street in Auckland, Allen Curnow. The lack of interest has to do with occasional writings in general, with festschrifts, bits and pieces, and that prejudice has been subdued by the present collection. All of his occasions conspire to make this an engrossing book. They are those of a New Zealand writer, and the foreign reader discovers here what it has been like to be one, to be this one in particular, a Kiwi agonistes.

In the course of a lecture of 1993 at the University of Otago he said that he hadn't 'really set out to be contentious on this occasion', but had possibly slipped into it. This brought a smile, all those thousands of miles away, when it turned up on the page. In London too, as in New Zealand, he is known to have been contentious. And in the Otago lecture, which occurred towards the end of the heyday of the delusional barrenness of literary theory, he'd only a moment before said that literary theory had been 'like an auto-immune

reaction, the cells of the body of literature attacking and destroying themselves'.

It's good that he has been contentious, willing to risk offence for good reason. In what has he offended? He is taxed here in interviews with being élitist (the All Blacks, he points out, are an élite), and with being polemical and 'abrasive', and I remember being at an Australian conference on literary journalism during the '80s and catching a murmur of this from the youthful New Zealand delegation. (Perhaps I should also declare that in an introduction to this book he describes me as abrasive in the sense of 'dour'. Scots people, even those who are as dour as budgerigars, get used to being called by that name. Stead remarks here that he is not thought, by those who know him personally, to live up to his reputation. This is true of Stead. And I keep saying it of myself.)

He is a keen New Zealander who believes that his country was parted from Britain by the British decision, in all its ambivalence, to enter Europe. No doubt the parting would have come about anyway. No doubt, either, that it is still incomplete, and may never be completed, and that there are New Zealand patriots who don't expect to live to regret this. He writes of his roots:

> We were not Englishmen. No one in my family, except one of my grandfathers, who was Swedish-born, had ever set foot in the northern hemisphere. Even my grandmother, who lived in the house with us, was the child of parents born in New Zealand. But in the cultural sense we were colonials.

He is neither unsophisticated nor bucolic, and his native Auckland is a city. But there are those in the cities of Western Europe and the

USA to whom this rootedness might appear archaic, as might his inwardness with crops and animals. It is hard not to think that this would be their loss, as would any comparable refusal of the Nova Scotian stories of Alistair MacLeod.

In a piece written in 1987 he returns to the matter of his roots in writing about the view from Mount Eden in Auckland. From the summit he can see 'most of the occasions of real significance in my life'. He was born down there, as were his parents, his wife and his children. A great-great-grandfather is buried there. His schools and his first university are there.

In his vivid and thoughtful novel of 1999, *Talking About O'Dwyer*, he revisits this view of his native ground, doing so in the person of the returned Oxford don Mike Newall, and evoking the scene with a rapture which might be experienced as nostalgic—Edenic, as you might say—by a reader who did not know that he is still there and not in that sense regretful. The novel is counterfactual—a little reminiscent of Henry James's 'The Jolly Corner', in which a man who has moved from one country to another wonders what he'd have been like if he'd stayed at home. The novel has several attractions—the feeling for women of various ages, and for battle. Not least is its equal or impartial feeling for New Zealand, England, Croatia, Crete.

He is not, then, a bigot about country. When he was a young New Zealander he thought that his native land and literature should declare their independence, and he worked for that, while well aware of what he owed to a participation in English literature. Colonial as he calls it, his participation can't

have been very different from my own, at the same age and at the same time, in Edinburgh, Scotland, so far as a place in the British Empire and a telepathic remoteness from the metropolis of London were concerned, and it's relevant to add that in the Scotland of the time secession could be considered by some, as it still is, though not by me, urgently desirable. Among his early influences were Rupert Brooke, John Buchan and Walter Scott. The first may be surprising; it's possible that the other two were no less mandatory in, as it were, Dunedin than they were in Edinburgh.

Now that New Zealand is more profoundly on its own, he has criticisms to make of it, which include the claim that a willed disconnection from the 'Anglo-Celtic' cultural heritage is proceeding. What he is against is the political correctness whereby, for instance, a respect for the Maori contribution to life in New Zealand—a contribution to which he is far from indifferent or hostile, as his recent novel bears witness—is demanded and enjoined. It's the demanding and enjoining he objects to in such instances.

During a conversation of 1996 on educational issues, his tenacious interlocutor Terry Locke asks a last question about 'what is currently shaping our identities as New Zealanders?' Stead replies: 'What's currently shaping our identity as New Zealanders, I suppose, is the attempt to shape our identity as New Zealanders.' This position belongs to a skein of argument to the effect that 'moralism' can be the death of art. The New Victorians are knocking at the door, he warns. He dislikes the requirement that writers write for useful purposes. He stresses the importance for literary discussion of an attention to language, and to the music it makes, as opposed to the morals to be found in books. But he wouldn't want to be reckoned an aesthete, not of the severer sort: he is a man who has morals, and strong opinions—about politics (his was a trade union family), and about rugby and soccer (he was once a centre-forward), and about books. There's a passage here which could be taken to disclose the moralist in him, and to indicate that political correctness can be both coercive and permissive:

> I'm not sympathetic to the idea of the English classroom as a place where people sit around expressing feelings and emotions and opinions. The emphasis in the classroom has gone over too far towards that, away from the student receiving information from an expert person who is a teacher.

The point could not be made more cogently.

The discussion with Locke peaks early when Stead charges his questioner with confusing different kinds of language: 'If I write a novel it hasn't any clear extraneous purpose other than to be a work of art in its own right, irrespective of what uses may be made of it. I don't see that to make that distinction is correctly described as "aestheti-cism", although aesthetics—the art of the novel—is relevant and important.' And it's true that *Talking About O'Dwyer* yields no unequivocal view as to whether the New Zealand-born should stay at home or settle in Oxford.

His treatment of the subject sometimes concurs, I think, with the new aestheticism which in recent years has become apparent in the work of such eminent critics as Harold Bloom and Helen Vendler, and which registers as a departure from, or rejection of, the moralistic critical approach now seen by some as an ancient dourness stored in the memory of the old. It is, in fact, by no means defunct. In abusive or degenerate form, it is accessible in the book pages of newspapers. It is part of what we do, readers and writers alike. And the abrasive Stead is against it, opposed to certain of its manifestations.

He is not in favour of discrimination on grounds of race or gender: in condemning interventions by politicians or teachers which are intended to stop this, he is merely saying 'that the way these policies *come into effect* can be legitimately questioned.' Novelists' interventions of this kind can also be ques-tioned. He argues that David Malouf's acclaimed Australian novel about a Caucasian hostility to Aborigines, *Remembering Babylon*, is a disappointment and that its final three paragraphs are poor. He quotes them, and they certainly seem to be. This doesn't mean that he is content with abusive behaviour towards Aborigines, and there are debates and conversations where the matter has to be spelt out.

The trouble for severe aesthetes is that satisfactory works of art can be shown to have, and to integrate, useful purposes, and that, to employ Stead's own terms, the existential self and the political self of a given individual are so often inseparable. Moralism is not new, moreover, and the current ways of putting it into effect tend to seem familiar. Textbooks and curricula are devised, as before, as ever, to serve useful purposes, some of which are more useful than others, just as some morali-ties are better than others.

The Chancellor of the Exchequer in the

British Labour Government has invited a wise man from America to address a seminar in which he is reported to have conveyed that single mothers should be locked up in institutions so that their offspring can learn virtue. This reaches back to the Victorian values of Mrs Thatcher's day, and to pre-Victorian values as well, and there could be no way of putting it into effect which would make it other than a bad idea. It has to be worse than calling for a law which forbids public expression of race hatred. The incarceration idea has been running for many years, let it be added, in the orphanages of Britain and Ireland, with effects which have come belatedly to light, and have revealed a staggering picture of cruelty and oppression. Meanwhile single mothers will continue to be stigmatised in Britain (though they won't be locked up), and race hatred will continue to be expressed and black people and white people to be killed for being black and white. This might encourage a certain tolerance of some forms of political correctness, bullying and sinister though it can seem at times.

I don't imagine, of course, that Stead has not thought about such complications. He also indicates that the morality of any state is likely to be complex and contradictory, in explaining that the enjoined orthodoxy of the political community in New Zealand is at odds with that of the country's teachers and writers: it seems that political correctness is not the only coercion to be aware of and to beware.

The discussion here of Ezra Pound, of whose poetry Stead is a conspicuously rational critic, is mostly biographical. Matters of paternity and maternity arise, as they do elsewhere in the book. Pound and his wife each had a child with an extramarital partner, a child who was given away to others to rear. Another essay recalls that Byron had a daughter—by Claire Clairmont—whom he sent to a nunnery, where she soon died. The essay speaks well of Claire Clairmont's letters and discusses whether or not (we still don't know) she had a child by Shelley, in whom, Stead writes, she recognised 'something noble'. Byron is blamed a little, but no one else is, from among these two sets of exiles in the aesthete's haven of nineteenth century Italy. It would be contentious to suggest that this forbearance was produced by aesthetic considerations. But it might be worth suggesting that a forbearance in relation to the vagaries of poet parents and poet spouses, and to other aspects of the ambiguous privacy of writers, has long been widely observed. The new morality came to notice by refusing to be bound by it, and confronting this or that celebrated writer with a citizen's arrest.

Canon Fodder
By Jan Cronin

Journal of New Zealand Literature 15, edited by Lawrence Jones and Heather Murray (University of Otago English Department, 1997) 166 pp., $25

In 1996 the University of Otago English Department hosted a conference entitled 'Curnow, Caxton and the Canon'. The Journal of New Zealand Literature undertook to publish selected papers, but found that the sheer volume of material merited two issues. As a testimony to the quality of the conference, the ensuing division into 'Curnow' and 'Caxton and the Canon' proves somewhat spurious; the Curnow issue (with which I am concerned) is extremely eclectic and revolves around him, rather than being uniformly focused on him. Yet what is intriguing here is that the devotion of an issue to Curnow evidently entailed more than the editors anticipated. That the project evolved into something unprecedented is evidenced by the absurdity of reviewing a textual object which can be known only as JNZL 15; 1997.

The apparently straightforward process of converting conference to text is complicated by Curnow's status as the patriarch of New Zealand poetry. It is insufficient somehow to merely collect a random group of essays, for his stature warrants a proportionate response. Or at least this is the tension discernible within the edition. Despite the sense that some of the essays remain essentially oral lectures, all are presumably aimed at publication on some level. The discrepancy arises from different conceptions of that publication and the attendant audience, something which the JNZL itself is obviously confused about. There are those who write with a sense of their own participation in the canon, writing into the cult of Curnow as it were, and those who, if they do not actually write against it, remain focused on the more immediate context of the conference. The tone of the issue is therefore uneven, oscillating between commemorative casebook and conference transcript.

Vincent O'Sullivan's '"About my father's business" or whose word is it anyway' constitutes the ideal opening piece—for a tribute that is—as it provides a sophisticated account of the complexity of the work, the versatility of the man, and his importance to New Zealand literature. Almost epic in scale, it situates Curnow on a continuum between Nietzsche and Baudrillard, and, one would think, provides an ideal departure for discussion of Curnow's work. There is, however, no such progression, and the apparent arbitrariness of the selection which follows suggests a lack of editorial input. While Noel Waite's 'Language, Poetry and Typography' is an elucidating if at times strained example of theoretical bibliographic studies, his primary focus on the Caxton Press renders him misplaced in this issue. In contrast to O'Sullivan's expertly polished piece, the tone of Waite's is ultimately exploratory and directed at a conference audience. The enterprise plunges towards absurdity with William Broughton's 'Curnow's anthologies and the strange case of William D'Arcy Cresswell', an antiphon to the awfulness of Cresswell's poetry, the point of which, despite its claim to 'consider . . . the possible significance of [Cresswell's] representation for the canonical process Curnow was undertaking', is the revelation of Curnow's personal integrity, his 'loyalty to another man's ideas'. Peter Simpson is clearly aware of such pitfalls. His piece bears the subtitle 'a documentary bibliography'. In other words it is no more or no less than what it claims to be, namely an account of the personal and professional relationship between Curnow and his printer Denis Glover. As such it is one of the most accomplished pieces, of genuine interest and worth. If Broughton's article can only be described as a curiosity, Simpson's aligns him with O'Sullivan and with the consolidation of the cult of Curnow.

Unlike some of the earlier pieces, it is clear why James Norgate's and Philip Armstrong's articles were included. Their juxtaposition represents a shift in emphasis from subject matter to critical approach. James Norgate's competent analysis of 'subversive Curnow' is an exercise in theoretical manoeuvring. Neither the argument nor the use of Bakhtinian dialogism are particularly innovative, but its merit for the editors lies in the application of one to the other. While Norgate's piece is ultimately too methodical to provide the required sense of a cutting edge, Philip Armstrong's consideration of Curnow's 'phenomenological colonialism' is lucid, compelling and deliciously self-conscious.

If the aim of the journal was to be a transcript of a conference, then there is nothing amiss in the lack of discernible logic in the juxtaposition of the first four essays. It is also fitting for the editors to provide a sense of the various critical approaches deployed. However when an agenda is suddenly inserted midway, it has two effects. The preceding material appears displaced, and the purpose of the enterprise becomes hopelessly diffused. With the final three essays it becomes apparent that the true site of contention is not Curnow, but contemporary critical practice in New Zealand.

John Geraets's 'Curnow / Curnow' is the most memorable piece for all the wrong reasons. It cries out for revision for textual presentation. It remains an oral delivery, the tone of which ranges from tongue-in-cheek to pretentious pontification. Geraets's principal aim is to 'unravel . . . the "decency" which Aotearoa literary practice has for too long

ravelled itself in'. To this end he occupies a number of outrageous positions. His central argument about the literary relationship (or lack thereof) between Curnow and son is, one hopes, a red herring, but there are uncomfortable moments where he takes it all too seriously. His essay is rife with the type of self-consciousness which continually trips over itself, as opposed to the subtlety of Armstrong's construction. Despite these flaws, Geraets's essay constitutes a challenge which the JNZL thought worth accepting, as the 'family romance' with which Geraets is chiefly concerned is not that of Curnow and son, but that generated by what he perceives as the oligarchic inclinations of the incestuous New Zealand literary community.

The brief editorial asserts that 'in addition we offer two papers on Curnow not presented at the conference, but which seemed important to include'. JNZL thus ditches the conference transcript model, and opts for the historical significance with which several of the writers seem preoccupied. JNZL has found itself almost by accident in the void where Allen Curnow criticism should be, and realises its potential too late. What would have made a crucial difference here is an introduction which articulates the status of the content and clarifies its readership, but unfortunately the editors appear to concentrate on removing themselves from the range of Geraets's attack.

John Bayley is a prestigious outsider, and part of his argument focuses on the implications of reading Curnow from that perspective. While he is refreshingly honest about what he terms the 'struggle' to comprehend Curnow's poetry, his essay concludes by reinscribing the nationalist paradigm of place in Curnow's existentialism, which it earlier dismissed as false consciousness. Alan Roddick's fine essay is similar enough in theme to provide the desired debate, and in terms of content, Geraets is rebutted by Bayley who is in turn rebutted by Roddick. Perhaps the most interesting element of Geraets's contribution is that while he advocates revolution, the context is that of the traditional debate between the local and the international, something which the juxtaposition with Bayley only confirms. The irony of it all is that beneath Geraets's theorised surface lies a more traditional sense of the mystical properties of literature, a sentiment which is echoed in the theoretical context of Bayley's work. Thus the JNZL, in rising to Geraets's bait, ends up trafficking in old school ideas rather than aligning itself with the more subtle theorising of Armstrong, and hence contracts where it hopes to expand.

JNZL has engineered something of a Frankenstein's monster, spawning a creature which, if it never fully understands itself, ultimately senses its own potential. While it is crippled by the limitations of the journal form, it highlights not only the need for a critical volume on Curnow (the only one in existence appears to be Roddick's contribution to the *New Zealand Writers and Their Work* series) and the availability of suitably high-class material, but also the anxieties which permeate contemporary critical practice in New Zealand.

subscribe
& sustain

LANDFALL

Two issues a year for $39.95. Or support the best New Zealand art and writing by becoming a **sustaining subscriber**. Friend: $NZ75–125; Patron: $NZ125 and above. For subscriptions, or for more information about the purpose and benefits of your **sustaining subscription**, contact:

University of Otago Press, PO Box 56, Dunedin fax 64 3 479 8385, email ‹ landfall@otago.ac.nz ›

MOVIES

Local Infections:
New Zealand Horror
By Philip Matthews

There are plenty of preposterous visual images in the Sam Neill/Judy Rymer-directed documentary *Cinema of Unease* (1995)—Neill feigns car sickness, Neill explains a Jaffa—but perhaps the nuttiest is the one in which Neill, re-enacting a boyhood memory of '50s Christchurch, rides his push-bike at a terrific clip past Sunnyside mental hospital. His face is partially covered by a handkerchief. He is dramatising a bourgeois fear of madness, a fear of contagion through exposure. Merely passing the hospital involved 'risking some kind of psychic infection'. This sequence is followed by a clip from Jane Campion's *An Angel at My Table* (1990)—Kerry Fox as a helpless, frightened Janet Frame in a hospital ward—with Neill suggesting on the voice-over that, as feared as madness was, it was also 'paradoxically, for many, the only way out'.

Now it's unlikely that Frame saw her misdiagnosis and the treatment that followed as an escape or a relief, but Neill is on to something, albeit tangentially. A given of horror movie theory is that horror films act as imaginative sites, psychological zones, in which society plays out its taboos and fears before re-establishing normality. The world is turned upside down. As Robin Wood put it in *American Nightmare*: 'One might say that the true subject of the horror genre is the struggle for recognition of all that our civilisation represses and oppresses: its re-emergence dramatised, as our nightmares, as an object of horror, a matter of terror, the "happy ending" (when it exists) typically signifying the restoration of repression.' However, normality tends to be 'boringly constant', and the monster suggests a secret wish to 'smash the norms that oppress us'. (Decades before the painfully self-conscious meta-horror film *Scream*, New Zealander Richard O'Brien's musical and movie, *The Rocky Horror Picture Show*, and its enduring cult following, was motivated by this knowledge of the rules of horror; *Picture Show*'s famous participatory screenings ran as an interactive, liberating fantasy in which the stifling normality of job/marriage/mortgage/death was magically undone by a demonic, seductive deviance.)

New Zealand has a thin tradition and short history of horror films, beginning with Sam Pillsbury's *The Scarecrow* (1982) and ending with Glenn Standring's brand new *The Irrefutable Truth About Demons* (2000). Excluding Peter Jackson's pre-respectability splatter films (*Bad Taste* (1986), *Meet the Feebles* (1990) and *Braindead* (1992)), which are comedies that satirise and demystify horror conventions rather than straightforward horror, and excluding Jackson's self-consciously 'grown-up', over-controlled *Heavenly Creatures* (1994), there have been highly derivative slasher films—David Blyth's *Death Warmed Up* (1984) and Scott Reynolds's *The Ugly* (1997)—and Garth Maxwell's strange, underrated, troubling art-Gothic *Jack Be Nimble* (1993). None of these films are world-beaters or field-leaders, but most have found an international audience on video, and they demonstrate a range of directorial ability from the apparently incompetent (Blyth) to the slick and heartless (Reynolds). What sets them apart, though, as examples of something like a 'national style' is the fact that they have nothing to do with the 'supernatural'. In these horrors, the monsters are humans—damaged, homicidal, psychotic. Neill was surely right to hurry past the madhouse, rather than the haunted house or the graveyard.

Shrouded in infernal steam, John Carradine's cadaverous Herbert Salter mumbles 'I am death' early on in *The Scarecrow*, but he is a frail, toothless image of death, easily defeated (killed in a light scuffle, buried at the town dump) and scarcely related to C. K. Stead's description of Salter in Ronald Hugh Morrieson's novel as 'Death the magician, clever and fascinating as well as horrible'. It's a casting problem, partly (Pillsbury seems uncomfortable with most of the darker aspects of the material), but there is also a way in which the character of Salter is less the demonic other, the grim reaper, than an almost unremarkable, natural extension of the entire male population of Klynham, an embodiment of the small town's tendencies towards casual brutality and sexual one-track-mindedness (everyone has a eye on Pru Poindexter, only Salter wants to kill her first). The source material is strong, and Morrieson's famous sentence—'The same week our fowls were stolen, Daphne Moran had her throat cut'—seems to summon up the entire landscape of small-town Kiwi Gothic, with its alcoholics and undertakers, itinerants and molesters. Against that line-up, good is represented by the Salvation Army, the temperance brigade, mothers with dinner waiting, upholding civilisation's thin veneer.

That's another world now, a bundle of clichés ready for Te Papa, but there is something in it that has become shorthand for a particular group of sensations. You see this, above all, in *An Angel at My Table* and Vincent Ward's *Vigil* (1984)—raw and elemental, as remote as a story from Genesis. Neither *Angel* nor *Vigil* is a horror film, but their sense of the Gothic has been hugely influential, feeding straight into the horror form. Frame's childhood experience, via Campion, is vivid enough to feel like a founding myth of New Zealand visual and literary culture, a collective unconscious. Somewhere back or beneath, this myth tells us, is a shared past marked by rural brutality, an opposition to difference and sensitivity, a widespread impoverishment of the spirit. That idea is so strong, and the expressionistic images so familiar, that some of *Jack Be Nimble*'s early scenes—young Jack silent and tormented at the dinner table of his adoptive family—are nearly replicas of scenes in *Angel*, as if to say that this is how we must express this stuff now, with dim light and a damp greyness and the constant threat of punishment. Other images in *Jack Be Nimble*—a boy whipped with barbed wire, a girl in a white nightie caught like a lamb on a barbed wire fence, a boy witnessing the killing of a pig as a double of himself—are so powerful and familiar that they too seem to have sprung from some collective well of rural Gothic. And they have a kind of truth: a news story about a boy whipped with barbed wire helped to inspire Garth Maxwell's screenplay, and one interviewer who worried about the gruesomeness of some of the film's images was pointed towards a story about 'a North Taranaki farming couple [who] used an electric cattle prod on their children while hanging them upside down from the back of the kitchen door'. Maxwell was keen to show that his film was as plausible as yesterday's news.

Maxwell has such a macabre sensibility, and his film has such a consistent, artful, anti-naturalistic style—mixing deep shadows, flickering sunshine, occasional heightened colour—that you end up wishing that his next project had been to remake *The Scarecrow*. His film has everything that Pillsbury's needed, hampered as the latter was by a jaunty tone and an inappropriate sense of modesty. What *Jack* also has—and this is a rare commodity in the New Zealand horror—is a sense of empathy. At its core, the film is about what happens when children who are tortured with cattle prods find the means for payback—'Damage the child and you damage the adult', Maxwell said at the time. What this does is to create a hero (the adult Jack, impressively played by American actor Alexis Arquette) who is every bit as unstable, unhinged and compulsively-programmed as any monster, and must also be dispatched before normality can be restored; people like him are not fit to wander about freely. But the film's horror scenario—perpetuated cycles of violence, routines of abuse, children and animals as property—is the very cycle of normality itself, as Maxwell kept pointing out, so no ending is really possible. *Jack Be Nimble* closes with all four of its male characters dead and one more male character waiting to be born, which is a far less triumphant happy ending than fantasy-based horrors tend to allow. (*The Scarecrow* also ends on an ominous or ambiguous note, with the news that the narrator's brother, who killed Salter, was 'changed' by the experience.)

Like the splatter films of Peter Jackson,

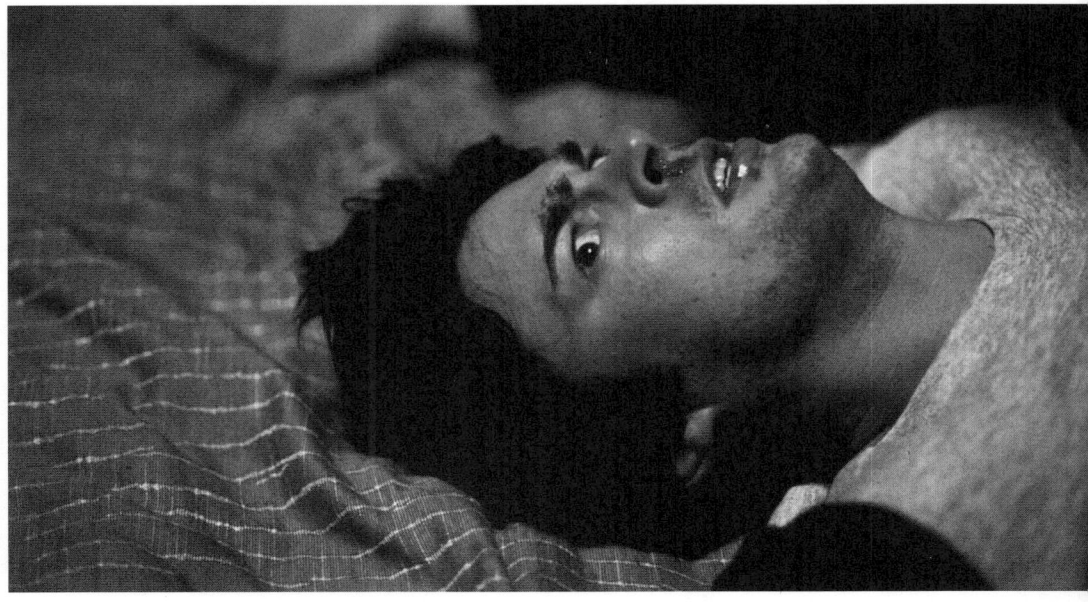

Karl Urban as Harry in Glenn Standring's *The Irrefutable Truth About Demons*.

Death Warmed Up and *The Ugly* are closer to fantasy, free of metaphor, and guided by the constraints of genre. The first is a seemingly randomly-assembled series of elements from '70s cult films—a motorcycles-in-a-tunnel sequence, a zombie sequence, a Cronenberg-esque mad doctor sequence—all done so clumsily as to seem like parody. The second is a serial killer film in an international tradition ('I used *Seven* quite a lot while making *The Ugly*,' director Scott Reynolds told *Sight and Sound*) and is effective within its conventions, but Reynolds's eagerness to make the Auckland locations come off as nowhere in particular can make the entire experience feel second-hand, anonymous, irrelevant. Only the killer's childhood—including a monstrous parent, isolation and humiliation, overcast suburban depression, the killer's nickname revealed as an abbreviation of 'the ugly duckling'—betray its New Zealand origins. Here we are again with a child, shaped by trauma, lashing out. And in both films, the mental hospital again figures as a prison for the criminally insane. But neither film feels truthful or plausible. Both films are movie films, movies about movies, movies that cannibalise movies.

And now *The Irrefutable Truth About Demons* takes up this poisoned chalice, this mixed history. The film could be said to exist in a conceptual space between *Fight Club* and *Hellraiser*, although it is not as original or as effective as either. It's an occult-based horror with an unreliable narrator and an untrustworthy point of view. A sceptical, cult-busting anthropologist (named Dr Harry Ballard, performed by Karl Urban) descends into a Satanic underworld, following the death of his brother, who was involved with the Satanists in question.

As a genre piece, *Demons* can be as grim, unsentimental and vicious as modern horror aficionados demand, with their freeze frames and fan sites, their connoisseurship of gore. But there are other considerations. Standring has obviously researched contemporary occult material—the tattooed hieroglyphs, the heavy-metal curses, the leather and piercings—and he is determined to use every last bit of it. Names such as Aleister Crowley are dropped, or conjured with, if you prefer, while, as the cult leader, Jonathon Hendry adopts the trademark look that '60s Church of Satan founder Anton LaVey handed down as the set uniform of cultivated, knowing 'evil'—the shaved head, the goatee, the black polo neck. At other points, there is a bloody crucifixion, approximations of torture, and a Manson Family-style slaughter scene, complete with bloody handprint and slogan. This fairly bent material, plus a largely nocturnal, urban setting and an accelerated, almost frantic, pace, give *Demons* the sense of a coherent nightmare world, of something oddly possible.

The tension in the film—as the *Fight Club* comparison indicates—is in whether the demons that pursue Harry are actual, tangible, physical, or whether they are paranoid hallucinations. Standring makes this idea explicit, too—demons are 'metaphors for our fears, for our guilt', Harry says, quoting the official scientific perspective—before blowing it all to hell, suggesting that demons might be metaphors and facts simultaneously, which makes a deliberate joke of 'irrefutable'. In other words, the film is a one-way ticket downwards, and those who find, as some do, that it appears to stop making sense are missing the point to some degree. The film is ultimately about the deliberate cultivation of madness, the wilful derangement of the senses. You could say that rather than hurrying past Sunnyside's gates, Standring is riding his bike directly through them. Mysterious things happen every time the hero smokes marijuana. Is *Demons* a stoner film about getting the fear? Standring has said that one inspiration was the 'feelings and experiences' triggered by a magic mushroom binge when he was a student. 'This friend and I made the mistake of taking too many, too many times, in the course of about a week,' he said. 'We literally fried our brains for, like, three months.' Naturally, this gave Standring an interest in schizophrenic perspectives. This lack of stability is the source of the film's horror. It's not a new trick, but it's almost always an effective one.

Demons closes in a mental hospital, but it ends with two impossible actions—a dead insect revived, a living person attacked by a dead person—that suggest an endlessness to the horror. The point seems to be that something that has been brought into the world can never be completely removed from it. No successful cure is possible, there is no 'closure' and no safety, the evil resides in memory and ideas even when its human agents are dead and gone. Protagonists are changed, perspectives gape disconcertingly, and nastiness flares time and again as if on some perversely looped film. This pessimistic point of view is the current engine of New Zealand horror—an evil that regenerates like Sam Neill's psychic infection, always unavoidable.

LOST AND FOUND*

Dusted Off:
John Hooker's Dunedin Gothic

By William Broughton

One of the side-effects of the publication of the *Big Smoke* anthology last year has been to remind us that experimental New Zealand writers in the '60s were provoked not only by an already established and vigorous local literature but also by a voracious interest in overseas journals. Chief among them was the New York periodical *Evergreen Review*, an avant-garde magazine that began publication in the later '50s and soon became acknowledged among a coterie of student readers in New Zealand as a place in which you could find the new, the jagged and the experimental. Someone described it to me recently as a magazine that 'gave off some great bohemian vapours' and there is, indeed, a telling photograph by Gary Baigent of a young Blair Smith, sitting below one of McCahon's 'Elias' paintings, holding the magazine like an ensign of Beat allegiance. Generously eclectic, the *Review* printed not only East and West Coast American work, but also English and (in translation) Continental writers, as well as some of the new Russian voices. In 1961 and 1963, it even accepted the work of a couple of New Zealanders.

I met John Hooker only once, during a visit

---

* In this regular feature, critics reconsider neglected works of New Zealand literature.

to Melbourne in 1967, when Ian Free, then a bookseller at the University Bookshop and formerly a linchpin of the old Paul's Book Arcade in Auckland, introduced us to each other as 'the only two New Zealanders to have published in *Evergreen Review*'. I had had one poem in *Evergreen* in issue 31 in late 1963, and John Hooker (b.1932) had a chapter of a novel in progress published under a pseudonym with the title 'Aughatane' in issue 16, the first issue of 1961, and he appeared there again in issue 28 in 1963 (the pseudonym, Hooker recalls, was his protection against draconian censorship laws; he also recalls that Aughatane was the name of a prize pig at the

Dunedin A & P Show in 1960). It may illuminate Hooker's achievement to note that other contributors to the issue included William S. Burroughs, Gregory Corso, Robert Duncan, Shelagh Delaney, and the sociologist C. Wright Mills. Hooker's novel finally appeared as *Jacob's Season* from the London publisher Barrie & Jenkins in 1971 and was reprinted by Penguin Australia two years later. It wasn't reviewed in *Landfall*, and receives only a one-line notice in Lawrence Jones's compendious survey of the novel in the *Oxford History of New Zealand Literature*. Rather like another Dunedin writer, John Sligo, who wrote some fine novels and novellas with eerily accurate South Island Gothic settings in the '70s, Hooker disappeared from our literary territory into the *ultima Thule* of Australia.

Yet *Jacob's Season* is a novel worth dusting off. If it hasn't been included in any of the canonical lists to date, then that is more the lists' fault than the novel's—a reminder that, even in a zealously revisionist period, vital work can slip through the nets of literary history. In *Jacob's Season*, Hooker evokes a semi-mythical and Gothic South Island, inhabited by characters who remind me of those in Baxter's mid-'60s plays or Frame's novel of the same years, *The Rainbirds*: marginal, lurching, comically desperate. Like those other two Dunedinites, Hooker's gift was to create characters who are utterly believable even when—especially when—they are most grotesque. *Jacob's Season* throngs with clowns at whose misfortunes we laugh because that is the only way not to cry at the pity of their foolishness.

Rereading the *Evergreen* piece and *Jacob's Season* this summer, I was struck by the delight of Hooker's characterisations, and by the way the novel enlarges and transforms the story, finding a place for its fragments in a larger grid of narrative, character, and event. His 'story' is experimental, choppy, deliberately fragmented, and its proximity in the *Review* to William S. Burroughs—master of the literary 'cut-up'—seems wholly appropriate. Hooker's piece in *Evergreen*, like Burroughs's, takes no pains to 'tell a story'. Rather it throws together glinting and acutely observed details, details unanchored by any central idea or persona. Nonetheless, a vision of loss and melancholy rises from the accumulated fragments. What 'Aughatane' does, moreover, is uncork Hooker's verbal inventiveness, and showcase his pitch-perfect ear for the registers of vernacular speech. Whether openly expressed or interiorised, the tedium and tragicomic despair of Hooker's speakers is richly present in their monologues and dialogues. These qualities give the extract a real vitality, even if, finally, there is a large hole in the piece where its narrative substance should be. 'Aughatane' confronts us with figures who are not fully-drawn characters so much as 'voices' in an expressionistic set piece that owes much to Joyce, Woolf, and, nearer to Hooker's time, J. P. Donleavy.

The novel is something else. It has focus and coherence, charm and poignancy, and a fine sense of the ridiculous. A short work, less than 45,000 words long, it has a stripped-down plot and races exuberantly through the life of its eponymous hero, propelled by all the skills of verbal contrivance that Hooker exhibited in the 'Aughatane' excerpt. Many of the images and speech-fragments from the story appear in the novel, but in the longer work they are embedded in more compelling fictional patterns—in a matrix of character and place that never threatens to dissolve.

For a start, the novel is *grounded*. Set in a brilliantly evoked late-provincial Dunedin, here renamed 'Flagstaff', *Jacob's Season* emanates a marrow-freezing chill. Hooker-country is Gothic to its core—a place of crumbling stone, knitted woollens, and dead leaves; a ghost-town. He nails the dampness, both spiritual and actual, of a city in which nineteenth century mercantile ambition has given way to echoes and winter mists. Those mists permeate the world of his sub-Rabelaisian anti-hero Jacob Small, bookseller, married man with family responsibilities, fornicator, drunkard and the architect—as the Calvinists of Dunedin would probably have it—of his own misfortune. As with Ronald Hugh Morrieson's Taranaki, the strangeness of Hooker's Dunedin is embodied in the language as much as it is evoked by any description of landscape or cityscape. Hooker plainly relishes the collision of Scottish settler dialect with the modern argot of a no-less-foreign popular culture, and his prose has a slangy gusto.

The embryonic excerpt in *Evergreen* has grown into a narrative that is, depending on your point of view, bitter-sweet or sadly humorous—the story of a loving and uxorious husband whose proclivities (sentimentality, drink, infidelity and unsaleable second-hand books) guarantee his fall. Jacob's world, commercial and marital, collapses under the weight of his own verbose capacity to deceive not so much those around him—his slatternly 'conquests', his long-suffering and excusably unfaithful wife, his cuckolder, or his grotesquely Dickensian employer—as himself. That 'verbose capacity', which makes the novel difficult to quote from except in paragraph-sized bites, is the very source of the characters' hold on us. Conversations run on and on, as every member of Hooker's menagerie surrounds him or herself with a carapace of words that can only fail as a protection against the appalling ordinariness of being alive. To everything there is a season, and for Jacob in this novel that season is winter.

After quitting New Zealand's literary scene, Hooker arrived at the centre of Australia's publishing world—a life that Jacob Small might have envied. Murray Waldren (see http://www.ozemail.com.au/ffiwaldrenm/hooker.html) has charted Hooker's eccentric path: the shift from Auckland University to the Dunedin of *Jacob's Season*; a 1962 residency amidst the 'dope and tarot cards' at Monterey University, California; circuitously, his arrival at Penguin as the flinty, boundary-breaking publisher of, among other things, *Portnoy's Complaint* and Anne Summers's *Damned Whores and God's Police*; and his return in 1985 to fiction-writing. Here in New Zealand, though, there doesn't seem to be have been any significant tribute to or even acknowledgment of *Jacob's Season*. Perhaps the decision to cross the Tasman put Hooker beyond the pale—another name to add to the list of 'ex' New Zealanders like Douglas Stewart and Bill Hart Smith. But even if 'history' judges Hooker solely on this one short book, it should record that he gave us a comic novel of some quality: vital, sharp-eyed, clearly (even unnervingly) 'local' in just the way that Ronald Hugh Morrieson was 'local', and above all compassionate in its delineation of human frailty.

FICTION

Our Impure Selections
By Russell Haley

Nineteen Widows Under Ash, Damien Wilkins (Victoria University Press, 2000) 309 pp., $29.95

A fiction writer's early work often preserves a spoor by which we can trace their current movements. In 1989, Damien Wilkins published a story, 'Out in the Field', in *Sport 3*. This short fiction reads oddly like the opening of a novel and, in many ways, it is a precursory run over the terrain now securely occupied by *Nineteen Widows Under Ash*. The key elements of that early story—the intrusion of a character's memories into the present, the character's absence from home, the dissolution of a marriage and the ensuing problems of child custody—all of these topics become major elements in Wilkins's mature fictions.

Damien Wilkins's latest novel is an eminently enjoyable book. His previous work of fiction, *Little Masters*, was an engaging novel too, but Wilkins's narrative abilities have matured considerably since that publication. *Nineteen Widows Under Ash* is the author's third novel and it is a particularly bold creation. My feeling is that there is a significantly large group of readers in this country who want to see our own manners and mores, this landscape and people, mirrored in our fiction. Wilkins, I am pleased to say, has sufficient literary confidence to head off into foreign territory and, I believe, he succeeds admirably in this overseas venture. Of course, he took a cast of characters to England and America in

Little Masters, but these people *were* young New Zealanders on their OE. The setting for *Nineteen Widows Under Ash* is the Pacific Northwest of the USA and, though there is an amusing flashback to Sri Lanka, the characters, landscape, dialogue and diction belong entirely to the United States of America.

Wilkins opens his novel *in medias res* and what seizes the reader from the outset is that Evelyn and Victoria, her daughter, are immediately present. Evelyn has left her husband, Denis, and she has taken their only child with her. She has been driving westward for fifteen hours in her Caprice Classic. Evelyn and the teenager argue about which radio station to listen to. Victoria, with all the perversity of a 'godless thirteen-year-old', wants to listen to a Christian Soft Rock station. Evelyn would rather tune in to the National Public Radio network.

There's a great deal going on in this apparently simple scene. The reader is situated immediately within one of the major concerns of this book: the mother and daughter relationship. Another, though less important, subject is touched on lightly—the nature of contemporary American Christianity. Issues surrounding Roman Catholicism in particular were also dealt with, largely sympathetically, in *Little Masters*. However, later on in *Nineteen Widows Under Ash*, Father Mullins is revealed as what used to be called a muscular Christian. He runs a Catholic booth at a tourist site and he's completely worldly. Father Ludlow is almost senile. And Father Andrew is deeply engaged in researching the history of the tonsure. Fundamentalists don't escape Evelyn's notice either. She sees a boy in a printed T-shirt. On the front, it says *Why is*

Satan Ugly as Sin. And on the back Evelyn reads: *Cos Jesus Beat Him With a Stick!*

Of course, we are looking at these things through Evelyn's eyes and she is certainly not a believer. Towards the end of the novel, she makes a definitive statement. "'God didn't make the world," said Evelyn. "Volcanoes did."' Any author takes risks when he or she presents the entire action of the novel from the point of view of a single character. Such a viewpoint is often unreliable; the reader has access only to what that one person experiences; our interest in that single individual may flag. We may not even like the central character. And Wilkins doesn't even allow himself that indirect authorial intervention where the writer can insinuate himself or herself into areas of free indirect speech. Evelyn's feelings and opinions, those private thoughts which remain unexpressed through dialogue, remain unmodulated by an authorial presence. In this third-person story the voice we hear is Evelyn's—not the writer's.

So some aspects of Evelyn's perceptions do appear to be flawed, less than humane. I'm thinking particularly here of Evelyn's attitude to a childhood acquaintance, Leonard Baird, who is otherwise known as Lenny or the Goose. There are moments when Leonard resembles a malign figure who might have escaped from a David Lynch film. Leonard Baird has had not only cancer of the throat but also a stroke. He makes ambiguous and somehow threatening telephone calls to Evelyn. It appears that he wants to involve her in the mercy killing of himself. But Evelyn also feels that this is what is desired of her by the elderly Catholic priest she looks after. Some of these scenes with Lenny and with Father

Vivian Ludlow take on a nightmarish quality, but Wilkins never really breaks with his chosen genre—family-realism.

Despite her shortcomings, Evelyn is a very engaging character. This woman has a splendidly sardonic tongue and her relationship with her daughter, Victoria, is brilliantly conveyed. Evelyn is staunch and she can be stroppy—witness the way she handles Denis, her cheating husband. Evelyn isn't a beautiful woman or even a conventionally attractive one. In her view her legs are too short. Her face is too rectangular, like a long box. And her hair isn't exactly a vivid colour; it's thin and rather mousy. Evelyn drinks and smokes, though she appears, significantly, to be giving up the habit towards the end of the novel.

But Evelyn certainly smoulders. So too does the mountain which is close to Evelyn Herbert's home town. Wilkins's fictional volcano is never named but we are in the Pacific Northwest. In 1980, Mount St. Helens in Washington State erupted so violently that millions of tonnes of ash were thrown twenty-five kilometres up into the atmosphere. The full name of Damien Wilkins's main character is Evelyn *Helen* Herbert.

So the symbolic structure of *Nineteen Widows Under Ash* is etched in, faintly but visibly, by the presence of the mountain and its possibly imminent eruption. In the course of the novel the Civil Defence warning in the area of the volcano moves from Alert 3 to Marginal 4. And what does that really mean? 'Jump ship', according to Evelyn. The seismic shudderings of the volcano are inextricably linked with the climax of the novel when Evelyn, together with her stepfather, Jerry, and another young woman are searching for the nineteen widows

of the title. The novel, by the way, has nineteen chapters.

The narrative form that Wilkins has employed in *Nineteen Widows Under Ash* is deftly handled. The time-shifts—an insignia of Wilkins's prose—work well, although when Evelyn thinks about her mother, Celia, the text becomes a little over-freighted with names and relationships. However, it is through these scenes from the past that we learn about Evelyn's extended family, and the profoundest human emotions, love and grief, are portrayed with exceptional skill. In short, the plot of *Nineteen Widows Under Ash* is splendidly submerged beneath the story. There are no obvious levers and pulleys in the novel and I applaud Damien Wilkins for this discretion. Changes in narrative direction spring from human failings and desires rather than from an imposed scheme. As the narrator of that early Wilkins's story notes: 'Plot is made of our impure selections, the dynamics of daily missed possibilities.' The 'impure selections' of his new novel deserve many readers, here and overseas.

PAPER CUTS

Boyzone

Anthologies are always trouble. In *Boys' Own Stories: Short Stories by New Zealand Men*, Graeme Lay has his work cut out for him. Lay kicks things off by evoking a new girl-pantheon—Chidgey, Knox, Kassabova, Perkins, Quigley, Neale—which 'has almost overshadowed' the ongoing productivity of their male counterparts. He acknowledges the influence of feminist politics in publication ('men, this argument goes, are merely getting a taste of their own rejection') and counters it ('others maintain that . . . it is men whose writing is on the endangered list'). He states that 'until now there have been no all-male anthologies' (what about *Best Mates?*). And he concludes, confusingly, that 'the art of short story writing in New Zealand is alive and well, regardless of gender, and that if there's such a thing as a literary contest between the sexes, the lads are holding their own' (the lads on the *Trainspotting*-orange cover are holding their own beers). There is potential juice in a discussion of crisis in New Zealand literature by young males, but any such discussion would need to have a sharper eye for the material and institutional life of literature (the perils of production, the lure of demographic marketing, the powers of our creative writing schools) than Lay exhibits in his strained and rather straining introduction; this book is too much in thrall to a corny vogue of 'dude literature' ('fiction written by men in their twenties and thirties') to bring any such crisis into focus. Lay rejects the Crumpie caricature of New Zealand masculinity as being 'not a

great advance on Cro-Magnon man', but the book supplants one cliché with another equally restricting. Simply, some contributions deal with laddish issues, some don't. Some of the stories depend for success on the anthology's framework, others transcend it. It's not *wholly* inappropriate to imagine the absurdity of an anthology called, say, *Blue-Rinse Ballads: Poems by Older New Zealand Women*. The most exciting writers in *Boys' Own Stories* (for my money, Michael Galvin, Bernard Steeds, Zion A. Komene, Duncan Sarkies, Phil Kawana, Chad Taylor, John McCrystal) deserve to be read unshadowed by modish themes. These, after all, are precisely the terms on which our contemporary female writing has come to maturity.

—Claire Murdoch

Corrugated Ironies

In the Bowen Gallery's recent publication, *Jeff Thomson Sculpture: 1992–2000*, there is a photograph depicting a pleasingly shabby seaside suburb—in the foreground a wooden bungalow with a corrugated iron roof. One among many, it was originally painted utilitarian green, but a large section of this roof has been replaced with brightly coloured iron screen-printed with motifs featuring marine flora and fauna. The old house is all dressed up like a surfie in a Hawaiian shirt. Jeff Thomson, sculptor, a.k.a. Jeff Thomson Roofing, has been at work putting the sunny side up. Well known for his ever-growing metal menagerie and his terrific station wagon in Te Papa, Thomson has begun to sling up chunky sample-sections of his roofs in art galleries, most recently the Bowen in

Wellington. To gallery-goers not familiar with the 'working roofs', the installation might recall the architectural vivisector, Gordon Matta Clark. But once you know of Thomson's roofing company the installation comes across as something more playful. At which point it's possible to be struck by two questions seldom asked in the same breath before: Is it art? And does it leak?

—Gerald Barnett

Collection Sandy McNeight, Wanganui.
Photograph: Leigh Mitchell-Anyon.

Jeff Thomson, *Roof*, 2000 (detail), screen-printed steel.

Bunker Mentality

What is it about shows of architecture in galleries? Even at their fullest and least cursory—Jean Nouvel at Wellington City Gallery, Alvar Aalto in Auckland—they back the art of building into a space halfway between the trade fair and the studio pinboard. *Screens*, an exhibition of 'investiga-tions and interpretations' by Victoria University architecture and design students up the hill at Wellington's Adam Art Gallery through the summer, failed in telling ways to extract itself from this particular corner. Executed in a predictably unpredictable range of materials and styles (from Chain-Link Bagel through to Shellac Attack) the students' screens were decisively overmastered by nothing less than the Adam Gallery itself. The Ian Athfield-designed building is a piss-elegant structure that—like at least one other New Zealand public gallery built in the '90s, and like many museums of the post-Frank Gehry period—seems geared less to display art than to advertise its own niftiness: the drama of its angled, slot-like spaces, the aromatically rubbery floors, the industrial swank of all those metal grilles and tracts of glass. (Though not as art-allergic as Te Papa, it nonetheless demonstrates a shift toward a style in museum building that might be dubbed 'Infinite Foyer'. Inspired by the aesthetics and ergonomics of the shopping mall, such galleries are all passage and no pause. It's enough to make one nostalgic for that much-maligned architectural form—the noble old white cube.) So, given that the building itself is as thorough a declension of the 'screen' idea as one could hope for, it was folly to hope that the students' small and mostly free-standing screens could survive the encounter. What's wanted is less caution and more vision in the liaison between buildings and exhibits. A show about building that went to work on the building itself—puncturing it, slicing it through, screening it out—now that'd be something to climb the hill for.

—Jeff Ford

LANDFALL 202

Out in November

true confessions / private lives

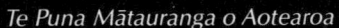

Te Puna Mātauranga o Aotearoa

NATIONAL LIBRARY
OF NEW ZEALAND

URSULA BETHELL

The first in a series of exhibitions on New Zealand poets

17 August – 18 November 2001

Ursula Bethell with cat Michael in the garden at Rise Cottage, 10 Westenra Terrace, Christchurch

Photograph by W.S. Baverstock
Collection of the Macmillan Brown Library
University of Canterbury

Gallery

National Library of New Zealand
Te Puna Mātauranga o Aotearoa
Molesworth Street, Wellington
Telephone: 0-4-474 3000

Gallery hours
9 – 5 Monday to Friday
9 – 4.30 Saturday
9 – 4.30 Sunday

The Long Dream of Waking

the centenary of *Len Lye*

30 June – 19 August 2001

A celebration of the life and work of this remarkable
artist. Kinetic sculptures, films, batiks, photograms
and paintings. A rare opportunity to see a
large part of this fabulous collection
at any one time.

Queen Street, New Plymouth info line 06 759 0850 Free entry Open 10.30 am-5pm

GOVETT-
BREWSTER
ART GALLERY

CHRISTOPHER WILLIAMS

TRANSFORM THE WORLD!
POETRY MUST BE MADE BY ALL!

SOLE NEW ZEALAND VENUE
28 APRIL - 17 JUNE 2001
SUPPORTED BY THE CHARTWELL TRUST
AND JENNY GIBBS TRUST AND MARGO
LEAVIN GALLERY LOS ANGELES

The Left Hand Raised

Peter Peryer
Photographs 1995-2001

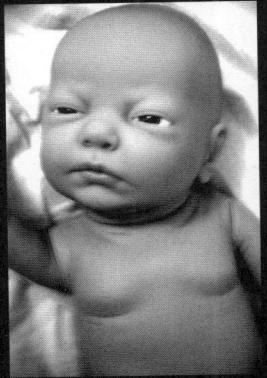

21 April - 24 June 2001

Queen Street, New Plymouth info line 06 759 0850 Free entry Open 10.30 am-5pm

GOVETT-
BREWSTER
ART GALLERY

UNDERWOOD
SASKIA LEEK
THIS MAY

UPCOMING
BRENDA NIGHTINGALE
HEATHER STRAKA
ANNE NOBLE
JUDY DARRAGH
LEIGH MARTIN
KRISTY GORMAN
LUISE FONG
MICHAEL PAREKOWHAI

JONATHAN SMART GALLERY

160 High Street, Christchurch, PO Box 22-554. Telephone: 64 3 365 7070
Fax: 64 3 377 5053 Hours: Wed - Fri 10.30am - 5pm Sat 10.30am - 1pm
e-mail: jsmart@caverock.net.nz
www.nzfineart.com

With this Ring

An offbeat look at marriage through intriguing objects and beautiful dresses

until 7 October 2001
[daily 10am - 5pm]

THE SCIENCE CENTRE & MANAWATU MUSEUM
Te Whare Pupuri Taonga o Manawatu

396 Main Street : Palmerston North : 06 355 5000

good work

the Jim Barr and Mary Barr Collection

DUNEDIN PUBLIC ART GALLERY

29 June – 26 August 2001

Ricky Swallow
Apple 2000 2000
pigmented resin and wire

30 the Octagon. PO Box 566 Dunedin
Ph 03 474 3240. Fax 03 474 3250
Email: dpagmail@dcc.govt.nz

A department of the Dunedin City Council

Man cannot understand without images.

St Thomas Aquinas

Peter McLeavey Gallery
147 Cuba St, Wellington

fiction of early **Landfall** contributors such as Bill Pearson, in the essays of past winners of this competition, and in the essays the journal continues to publish.

The Prize and the Issue

The winning essay will be published in **Landfall 203**, May 2002. This, with the best of the short-listed essays, will form a **special New Zealand non-fiction feature** in the same issue. **A prize of $2500 goes to the winner.**

The winner will be notified by telephone.

the **LANDFALL** essay competition

Conditions of Entry

1   Essays will be fully developed, independent works and will be no more than 6000 words long.
2   Essays will be on a topic of the author's choosing.
3   Essays will not have been published elsewhere.
4   Writers will be resident in New Zealand.
5   One entry per person will be accepted. Entrants should include a stamped, addressed envelope for return of their contributions.
6   The judge will assess the merits of the essays and reserve the right not to award a prize. No correspondence with the judge will be entered into.
7   **Landfall** reserves the right to publish the winning entry, and other short-listed entries, at the editor's discretion.
8   It is a condition of the competition that the winning writer's name and photograph may be used by **Landfall** for publicity purposes.

How to Enter

1   Manuscripts should be supplied in hard and soft copies, with text saved as MS Word or text-only files on a 3.5' floppy disk.
2   Two hard copies of manuscripts are required. These should be typed with double-line spacing and wide left-hand margin.
3   The name, address, and telephone number of the author should appear on a separate sheet of the manuscript.
4   Entries must be received by 5pm, December 21, 2001.
5   Send entries to:

Landfall Essay Competition
University of Otago Press
PO Box 56
Dunedin

CONTRIBUTORS

Laurence Aberhart is a self-taught photographer. Born in Nelson in 1949, he discovered photography in 1968 and has been in thrall to the medium ever since. He visited Toi Shan, China, in November 2000 while on a residency with the Macau Art Museum. His Macau photographs will be exhibited at the Macau Art Museum between August and November 2001.

Margaret Atwood's newest novel, The Blind Assassin, won the prestigious Booker Prize in 2000. Atwood is the author of more than twenty-five volumes of poetry, fiction and non-fiction. The recipient of numerous awards and several honorary degrees, she is perhaps best known for her novels, which include The Edible Woman (1970), The Handmaid's Tale (1983), and Alias Grace (1996). Atwood currently lives in Toronto with novelist Graeme Gibson.

Lita Barrie is an expatriate New Zealand art critic and feminist writer based in Los Angeles, where she is a lecturer at California State University and a visiting lecturer at Art Center College of Design and Claremont Graduate School.

Paola Bilbrough's first collection of poetry, Bell Tongue, was published by Victoria University Press in 1999. Later this year she has a residency at Keio University in Tokyo where she will continue work on a novel.

Ellen Brooks is a photographer based in New York. A graduate of the University of California, she was a guest artist at the Art Institute of Chicago in 1999 and a recipient of a McDowell Residency in 1998. Her work has been seen in many exhibitions in America and Europe, most recently in a solo exhibition at Leslie Tonkonow Gallery, New York, in 2000, and in the group exhibition The Snapshot, at Baltimore Museum of Contemporary Art.

William Broughton has taught English at Massey University, Palmerston North, since 1963. His special interest has been mid-twentieth century New Zealand literature.

Jonathan Bywater teaches in the Design School at Unitec in Auckland and writes regularly for LOG Illustrated and Art New Zealand.

Kate Camp is a Wellington poet. Her first collection Unfamiliar Legends of the Stars won the Best First Book Award at the 1999 Montana New Zealand Book Awards. A second collection, Realia, will appear in June 2001 from Victoria University Press.

Janet Charman lives and works in Auckland.

Jan Cronin is a foundation scholar of Trinity College, Dublin, and will soon begin a Ph.D. about New Zealand literature at Leeds University.

Mike Davis's City of Quartz: Excavating the Future in Los Angeles (1990) was recently selected by the San Francisco Chronicle as one of the 'ten best books written about the American West in the twentieth century'. More recently, Davis has published Ecology of Fear: Los Angeles and the Imagination of Disaster (1998), Magical Urbanism:

Latinos Reinvent the U.S. Big City (2000) and *Late Victorian Holocausts: El Nino Families and the Making of the Third World* (2001). He lives, whenever he can, in Papaʻaloa, Hawaiʻi.

Jane Gardner is a Wellington writer who attended Victoria University's Creative Writing Course in 1995. Her poetry has appeared in *Sport*, *Mutes & Earthquakes*, and in various New Zealand Poetry Society publications. 'Cowgirl in the Sand' is her first published story.

David Glynn was born in Auckland. He was awarded the Vintage 10th Anniversary Scholarship in May 2000. *Drownland* will be published by Vintage.

Russell Haley lives in the countryside north of Auckland. He has held the ICI Writing Bursary, the University of Auckland Literary Fellowship, and the Katherine Mansfield Fellowship in Menton. His most recent book, *A Spider-Web Season and The Transfer Station*, was published by Hazard Press in 2000. A new novel, *Tomorrow Tastes Better*, is due from HarperCollins in August 2001.

Bernadette Hall is a poet and playwright who lives in Christchurch. In 1997 she represented New Zealand at the International Writers Community in Iowa, USA, where she became a close friend of the Ugandan novelist, Goretti Kyomuhendo. Halls's fifth collection of poems, *Settler Dreaming*, produced in collaboration with Dunedin artist, Kathryn Madill, is due out from Victoria University Press later this year.

Jeffrey Paparoa Holman is a student in the English and Maori departments at Canterbury University, researching the bicultural critiques of Bill Pearson. His second book of poetry, *Flood Damage*, was published by Nga Kupu Press in 1998. His work has appeared in *Poetry Wales*, *Landfall*, *Sport*, *Takahe*, *North & South* and the *Listener*.

Andrew Johnston lives in Paris where he works for the *International Herald Tribune*. 'As, When, While' was written as the epigraph to a doctoral thesis in linguistics on these three words, by Rosalind Dilys.

Anne Kennedy's last book was the novel *A Boy and His Uncle* and her most recent script project was the screenplay of Dorothy Porter's *Monkey's Mask*.

Tessa Laird is a New Zealand writer and former editor of *LOG Illustrated*. Tessa is currently residing in Los Angeles, where she works as an internet lexicographer and builds her website in her spare time (www.fusionanomaly.net/tessa). Despite the multifarious attractions of LA, Tessa regularly dreams of a home in New Zealand.

Saskia Leek is a painter based in Auckland. Her work has recently featured in the exhibitions *Ghost Painting* (Dunedin Public Art Gallery, 2000), *Glorious Dreams* (Govett-Brewster Art Gallery, 2001) and in *Bright Paradise* at the Auckland Art Gallery in 2001.

Douglas Lloyd-Jenkins has published widely on New Zealand architecture and design. The curator of recent exhibitions about Avis Higgs and William Mason, he is Associate Professor at the Unitec Design School in Auckland.

Philip Matthews is a writer with the *Listener*, where his award-winning film criticism has appeared since 1994.

Roger McDonald is the author of six novels: *1915*, *Slipstream*, *Rough Wallaby*, *Water Man*, *The Slap* and *Mr Darwin's Shooter*. His account of his travels with New Zealand shearers, *Shearer's Motel*, will soon be republished by Random House.

Cilla McQueen's seventh book, *Markings*, was published in July 2000. She lives and writes in Bluff where she is working on another book of poetry. A selected poems is due this year from University of Otago Press.

Felicity Milburn lives in Christchurch and is currently the curator of contemporary art at the Robert McDougall Art Gallery.

Karl Miller founded and edited for many years the *London Review of Books*. He has also been the Literary Editor of the *Spectator* and the *New Statesman*, as well as Editor of the *Listener*. From 1974 to 1992, he was the Lord Northcliffe Professor of Modern English Literature at University College, University of London. His books include *Cockburn's Millennium*, winner of the James Tait Black award, *Doubles*, and two volumes of autobiography, *Rebecca's Vest* and *Dark Horses*.

David Mitchell is an architect and writer based in Auckland.

Emma Neale has a Ph.D. from University College, London. She has published a novel (*Night Swimming*, Vintage, Random House New Zealand, 1998, Anchor, Transworld, Australia, 1999) and a volume of poetry, *Sleeve-notes* (Godwit, Random House, New Zealand 1999). Her second novel, *Little Moon*, is due out from Random House New Zealand this year. She is currently the recipient of the Creative New Zealand/Todd New Writer's Bursary.

James Norcliffe has published *The Chinese Interpreter* (short stories), three collections of poetry, most recently *A Kind of Kingdom* (Victoria University Press), and a number of novels for children. He was the 2000 Robert Burns Fellow at the University of Otago. Recent work has been published in *Sligo*, *Tabla Book of New Verse*, *Staple* and *Stand*.

Gregory O'Brien co-edited, with Louise White, *Big Weather: Poems of Wellington* (Mallinson Rendell, 2000) and is currently curating an exhibition of paintings and prints by John Drawbridge for City Gallery, Wellington.

Chris Price is the immediate past editor of *Landfall*, as well as being Writers and Readers Coordinator for the New Zealand Festival. In the second half of this year she will teach a course on 'Creative Writing in the Marketplace' at Victoria University.

Nicholas St John lives in Wellington, where he works as an actor. He uses a nom de plume because of his deep admiration for rock stars with invented names. He is unsure if he will ever grow out of it, though he is still quite young.

Iain Sharp edits the books page for the *Sunday Star-Times* and works in the Special Collections of Auckland Public Library.

Laurence Simmons is Head of the Department of Italian and a member of the Department for Film, Television and Media Studies at the University of Auckland. He has a strong interest in contemporary theory and has written widely on contemporary New Zealand art and film. His most recent publication (together with Heather Worth) is an edited volume of essays entitled *Derrida Downunder*.

Damian Skinner is currently undertaking a Ph.D. in art history at Victoria University in Wellington.

Ian Wedde was born in 1946, and never really recovered from unprotected contact with Bluenote vinyl and the French symbolist poets.

Peter Wells is a film-maker and author, and was co-winner of the 1999 *Landfall* Essay Competition. He writes: 'During the late Nazi era, cyanide capsules were placed in the back teeth—useful for troubling moments, a sort of apocalyptic Mintie. This year I am bringing out my memoir. In a closed, fetid, faintly hysterical, and morbidly secretive society, the Mintie idea has some appeal.'

Damien Wilkins's most recent novel is *Nineteen Widows Under Ash* (Victoria University Press), reviewed in this issue.

Rhys Williamson lives in Tauranga and works in the horticulture industry.

ACKNOWLEDGEMENTS

For their suggestions and assistance, thanks to Kathryn Carmody, Yvonne Todd, Mary Trewby, Peter Wells and Mark Williams.

For his energy and generosity, thanks to *Landfall*'s outgoing designer, Aaron Richardson. Since its earliest issues, *Landfall* has aimed to combine words that count with design that works. Aaron's redesign of the journal, launched in *Landfall* 200, didn't just live up to that tradition. It shook it awake and took it somewhere new. Aaron designed the current issue with *Landfall*'s new designer, Bepen Bhana of *designworks*.